P.S. to Operating Systems

P.S. to Operating Systems

Larry Dowdy
Craig Lowery

*for ACM SIGMETRICS
and the Computer Measurement Group (CMG)*

PRENTICE HALL, Englewood Cliffs, NJ 07632

Library of Congress Cataloging-in-Publication Data

Dowdy, Larry.
  P.S. to operating systems / by Larry Dowdy & Craig Lowery.
    p. cm.
  Includes index.
  ISBN 0-13-011685-8
  1. Operating systems (Computers)--Evaluation. I. Lowery, Craig.
  II. Title.
  QA76.76.063D695 1993
  005.4'3--dc20
                                    92-37386
                                       CIP

Acquisitions editor: **WILLIAM ZOBRIST**
Editorial/production supervision and
  interior design: **RICHARD DeLORENZO**
Copy editor: **BARBARA ZEIDERS**
Cover design: **RAY LUNDGREN**
Prepress buyer: **LINDA BEHRENS**
Manufacturing buyer: **DAVID DICKEY**
Editorial assistant: **DANIELLE ROBINSON**
Supplements editor: **ALICE DWORKIN**

© 1993 by Prentice-Hall, Inc.
A Simon & Schuster Company
Englewood Cliffs, New Jersey 07632

The author and publisher of this book have used their best efforts in preparing this book. These
efforts include the development, research, and testing of the theories and programs to determine
their effectiveness. The author and publisher make no warranty of any kind, expressed or implied,
with regard to these programs or the documentation contained in this book. The author and
publisher shall not be liable in any event for incidental or consequential damages
in connection with, or arising out of, the furnishing, performance, or use of these programs.

Printed in the United States of America

10 9 8 7 6 5 4 3 2 1

ISBN 0-13-011685-8

Prentice-Hall International (UK) Limited, London
Prentice-Hall of Australia Pty. Limited, Sydney
Prentice-Hall Canada Inc., Toronto
Prentice-Hall Hispanoamericana, S.A., Mexico
Prentice-Hall of India Private Limited, New Delhi
Prentice-Hall of Japan, Inc., Tokyo
Simon & Schuster Asia Pte. Ltd., Singapore
Editora Prentice-Hall do Brasil, Ltda., Rio de Janeiro

Contents

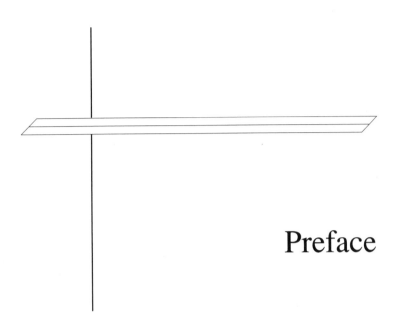

Preface

The goal of this book is to increase the performance awareness and to improve the performance modeling skills of computer science and computer engineering students. Often, performance issues are ignored ("That's someone else's job"), given secondary status ("Let's get it working first and then we'll tune it by tweaking a few knobs if it runs too slowly for the boss"), or are treated as an isolated topic ("That's treated in Chapter 13 and can be omitted if time doesn't permit" or "That's treated in course CS284, which is too mathematical and is optional anyway"). Another viewpoint is taken here: Performance issues are sufficiently important to be incorporated in and throughout every computer-related course.

In this book we focus on selected operating systems issues. The title *P.S. to Operating Systems* is an acronym for *Performance Supplement to Operating Systems*. It serves as a reminder to "Hey, guys, don't forget about performance concerns!" when studying, designing, or comparing the various aspects within operating systems. This book contains supplemental material intended to augment existing material (e.g., texts) on operating systems. It is not intended to replace any operating systems text since many key issues inherent to operating systems are not covered here. Neither is it intended to be the basis for a first course in performance evaluation, since many important issues and techniques within that field have also been ignored. Rather, we have tried to compile a sequence of interesting operating system problems, through which some basic performance evaluation techniques can be described and applied.

The level of presentation is appropriate for a beginning course in operating systems (e.g., a junior-level college student). Very little prerequisite information is assumed. A general knowledge of computers and computer terminology is needed. The presented examples are quantitative, so basic mathematical skills are assumed, but certainly anyone with a basic knowledge of calculus and linear algebra will not have difficulty. Many instructors of introductory operating systems courses are not "performance persons." Therefore, special attention has been given to make the presentation self-contained and straightforward. All discussions have been built up from first principles, so the reader does not have to be concerned that something will be thrown in that must simply be taken on faith.

This book is based on examples and applications. The typical scenario followed is first to pose an interesting problem. The examples chosen are neither trivial nor theoretically abstract. Ideally, the reader would say "Gee, that's an interesting problem that (1) I could see myself faced with someday, and (2) I have no idea how I would go about solving it." Based on this motivation, an in-depth solution approach is followed. Along the way to solving the problem, appropriate solution techniques are naturally "discovered." Our intention is not to trick or impress the reader to the point where, after going through a problem, the reader says "That was really a clever way to solve the problem," meaning "I never would have come up with that solution on my own." Instead, it would be a success if the reader, after going through a problem set, would say "That was easy—I should have known that already—give me another problem like that and I'll show you I can solve it myself." Thus in hindsight, if a reader thinks that this book is lacking in new solution tricks, that's okay.

The series of examples is progressive, even though this may not be immediately obvious from the problem statements. That is, the problems addressed may appear to be disjointed, but the techniques to be discovered and used during the problem solutions build on the techniques presented in earlier problems. The same is true for the exercises given at the end of each section. These exercises are not an afterthought and are not given simply to reinforce the immediately preceding material. Several of them are quite challenging and bring out subtleties not addressed in the prose. A scheme of asterisks is used to rate each exercise with respect to difficulty and the estimated completion time. A single asterisk indicates that the problem is "simple" and should take a minimum amount of time to complete. Two or three asterisks indicates that the problem is more challenging, requiring a good working knowledge of the techiques used in the chapters. Four asterisks indicates that the problem is quite challenging, requiring either a fair amount of time and/or computer aid such as writing a program or using packaged software. These exercises are inherent to the book's development.

The writing style is "down home," very simple and direct. We want this to be light reading that is informative and useful but at the same time, fun. (This is the way things are done in Tennessee. Others may refer to this style as "corny" and nonprofessional. To such people we are apologetic, yet unashamed.) As interesting tangents arise, they are explored. When sticky issues arise, or when the tangents begin to lead too far afield, an abrupt shift back to the main issues will result. The writing style relies heavily on analogies. This is because computers are, frankly, often boring things to talk about. Therefore, instead of processors and processes, waiters and customers at a burger joint are used. Instead of scheduling jobs on processors, scheduling the use of a VCR to view movies are described. Instead of comparing various disk scheduling strategies, various alternatives to servicing broken-down machinery are compared. The mapping to the corresponding operating system issues will be clear. The use of boxes allows important issues to be repeated or reinforced and presented in a different form.

> Like this.

We have found this Jekyll/Hyde, or good cop/bad cop, mechanism to be quite useful in many situations.

This book is available in LaTeX[1] form, the motivation being that the book can easily be customized and reproduced. For example, instead of talking about machine X, which has no personal meaning to the students at a particular university, machine *Lil' Nellie* can easily be substituted. Instead of poking fun at *generic person X* it is possible to substitute *specific person Y*. Also, the instructor may want to edit out portions of particular problem solutions and assign them as exercises. Later, these problems can easily be reproduced with the complete solutions edited back in to provide a solution set. This also allows the instructor to delete and/or add individual pet problems.

> Thus every college, university, or other institution can have its own personalized book simply by contacting its Prentice Hall representative.

This book is the first in a series of performance supplements. Others which are planned include *P.S. to Computer Architecture, P.S. to Computer Networks, P.S. to Software Engineering, P.S. to Database Systems, P.S. to Distributed Systems*, and *P.S. to Programming Languages*.

This book results from a project sponsored jointly and equally by the Computer Measurement Group (CMG) and the Association for Computing Machinery's Special Interest Group on Measurement and Evaluation (SIGMETRICS).

---

[1]LaTeX is Leslie Lamport's macro package for use with Donald Knuth's TeX typesetting program. Both LaTeX and TeX are freely available. TeX is a trademark of the American Mathematical Society.

The original idea was simply to obtain a collection of exercises from a variety of sources (i.e., people), standardize the notation, and then loosely compile them in book form. As the exercises came in, it was immediately clear that putting the exercises together into anything that would flow naturally and logically was (how shall we put this?) not quite as easy as originally planned. The final result is that as the exercises came in, topic themes were abstracted. The original exercises were rewritten to the extent that the original contributors will not even be able to recognize their contributions. Apologies are in order. However, we believe that the final result is a better and more useful product. With this said, the following list of individuals are the real contributors who deserve credit for helping to make this project possible.

Ashok Agrawala	Bill Hooper	Herb Schwetman
Andre Bondi	Chuck Hopf	Ken Sevcik
Rick Bunt	Tom Keller	Evgenia Smirni
Brian Carlson	Ken Kolence	Y.C. Tay
Cindy Childers	Ed Lazowska	Satish Tripathi
Bernie Domanski	Leo Lo	Kishor Trivedi
Derek Eager	David Nicol	Mary Vernon
David Finkel	Dan Reed	Tommy Wagner
Mark Holliday	Emilia Rosti	John Zahorjan

the fall 1990 class of CS281 at Vanderbilt University

We sincerely thank and acknowledge the contributions and support of each of these people. As a final note, we acknowledge the use of several software aids. These include LaTeX, Maple, SPNP, and GreatSPN[2]. Comments, corrections, and/or suggestions are appreciated and may be directed to:

Larry Dowdy,
Craig Lowery,
Department of Computer Science
Vanderbilt University
Nashville, Tennessee 37235
email: lwd@vuse.cs.vanderbilt.edu

---

[2]Maple is the proprietary symbolic algebraic package developed by the Symbolic Computation Group, University of Waterloo, Ontario, Canada. SPNP (Stochastic Petri Net Package) is a package for solving stochastic Petri networks developed by Kishor S. Trivedi et al., Duke University, Durham, North Carolina. GreatSPN is a graphics interface-oriented package for the solving and simulation of stochastic Petri networks developed by Gianfranco Balbo and Giovanni Chiola at the University of Torino, Torino, Italy.

P.S. to Operating Systems

chapter one

System Design I: Single Station

PROBLEM

Mr. K is the manager of a new Snowball Express sno-cone stand which will soon be opening for business. The stand is operated by a single attendant who sits behind a window. People come up to the window, tell the attendant which flavor sno-cone they want, wait for the attendant to fill their order, then pay and leave.

In operating systems terminology, the attendant is the CPU and the arriving people represent the workload submitted.

When there is more than one customer at the window, a line forms so that customers are served in the order that they arrived. People always buy one and only one sno-cone at $3 each. The cost of materials to make sno-cones is negligible, so Mr. K considers all of the money taken in to be profit, except that the attendant has to be paid from the money received. A picture of the sno-cone stand is shown in Figure 1.1.

After interviewing several applicants for the attendant's position, Mr. K has narrowed his choice to two people: Fran and Bill.

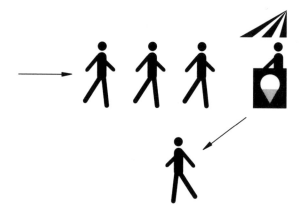

Figure 1.1   The Sno-Cone Stand

> The operating systems counterpart is to choose between two CPUs of vary-
> ing costs and speeds.

Mr. K has discovered (during the interviews) that Fran can complete a transaction (take the order, make the sno-cone, take payment, and make change) in 20 seconds on the average. Bill can perform the same job in 30 seconds on the average. Fran is faster than Bill but demands $12 per hour in wages, whereas Bill will work for $6 per hour.

Market research has revealed that, on the average, Mr. K can expect one customer per minute to come up to the window.

> This represents the workload characterization phase.

Mr. K has also learned that his prospective customers are the kind that do not like to wait in long lines. If a customer comes to the window and there are already three people in line, he or she will promptly turn about in a huff and storm off to the Smoothy-Cream, a nearby competitor.

> The buffer size is assumed to be three.

Taking all of these facts into consideration, which person is the more cost-effective to hire: Fran or Bill?

The objective function is to maximize profit, which is the difference between extra money earned by having a faster processor and the cost of having a faster processor.

1.1 APPLICATION TO OPERATING SYSTEMS

Modern multiprogrammed computer systems comprise several devices from which processes (i.e., jobs) receive service. For example, a process may require computation service from the central processing unit (CPU), then input/output (I/O) service from a disk, and so on. Since the computer system is multiprogrammed, there are usually several processes competing for the same resources. For example, more than one job may wish to use the CPU at the same time.

In this problem, the sno-cone-stand attendant is analogous to one device (also called a "station" or "server") in the computer system, and the customers wishing to buy sno-cones are analogous to the processes demanding service from that device. The maximum line length of three is analogous to a device that has a limited amount of "waiting" space, where processes wait until they can be served by the device.

This is also referred to as a finite-length queue or buffer.

In the design of a computer system, choices have to be made. The choice here is: Do we use a slower but cheaper device, or a faster but more expensive device? The decision is based on several things. How much demand will be placed on that device? Will the improved performance yielded by the faster device offset its additional expense?

1.2 SOLUTION

Fran is 33% faster than Bill, yet to employ Fran costs 100% more than to employ Bill. This seems to imply that Bill is the better choice. However, this natural intuitive reasoning is not always correct. Specific quantitative reasoning is needed. In order to choose Bill over Fran, we must be able to make and back up such statements as the following:

> The amount of money made while Fran operates the stand minus her pay is less than the amount of money made while Bill operates the stand minus his pay. Therefore, Bill is the better choice.

> Or, in the operating systems scenario, the improved throughput with a faster processor does not offset the extra cost of that processor.

How can such a statement be supported? The first step is to identify the quantities of interest:

1. Amount of money made while Fran works
2. Amount of money made while Bill works
3. Cost to employ Fran
4. Cost to employ Bill

In order to make calculations and comparisons with these figures, the quantities they represent must all be with respect to the same unit of time. It does not really matter what standard unit of time is chosen. What is important is that once the unit is chosen, all measurements are converted to reflect that unit. The problem above suggests *second*, *minute*, or *hour*. Arbitrarily, 1 minute is selected as the standard time unit. The statement we now wish to prove (or disprove) is:

> The average amount of money made each minute while Fran operates the stand minus her pay per minute is less than the average amount of money made each minute while Bill operates the stand minus his pay per minute. Therefore, Bill is the better choice.

Fran's and Bill's pay per minute are easily obtained by dividing each hourly payrate by 60. Fran makes $12 per hour (i.e., 20 cents per minute) and Bill makes $6 per hour (i.e., 10 cents per minute). These are the latter two of the four quantities required.

We now need to calculate the average amount of money taken in for each minute that each attendant works. Although the customers will come to the sno-cone stand at the same rate regardless of who is working, they are more likely to find the line of an acceptable length (fewer than three people in line before they get into line themselves) if Fran is working than if Bill is working.

> The buffer length is an important parameter and must be considered.

(Remember that if the line is of length three, potential customers turn away and go to Smoothy-Cream, and that results in lost revenue.) This is because Fran is faster than Bill (on the average) and will be able to handle more customers, thus keeping the line length shorter. So, ultimately, the amount of money taken in each minute depends on the average number of customers that are actually served every minute.

> The $3 cost per sno-cone is a scaling factor for throughput in this problem. In the operating systems scenario it is the weight given to a completed job relative to the negative cost of providing service.

But does the amount of extra money made when Fran works (due to customers not going to Smoothy-Cream) offset the extra cost of employing her over Bill?

Let's first assume that *exactly* one customer arrives *every* minute, on the minute. Let's also assume that Fran can service each customer in *exactly* 20 seconds, and that Bill can service each customer in *exactly* 30 seconds. Then, obviously, the line will never grow longer than one person, that being the person currently being served, regardless of whether Fran or Bill works.

> That is, if we assume that the distributions of interarrival and service times are constants, Bill is the better choice.

If we made these assumptions—that the average customer arrival rate and the average service times are the same exact values for every customer—we would certainly advise Mr. K to hire Bill. Bill will get exactly one customer every 60 seconds, but he only needs exactly 30 seconds to take care of each customer. This leaves exactly 30 seconds out of every minute in which Bill can goof off, because there will be no one waiting in line.

> With these assumptions, the throughput using either CPU would be the same. That is, the CPU unit is not the bottleneck and it would be best to select the cheaper, slower CPU.

As a matter of fact, there will never be a line—only the one customer being served (half the time). Since no customer will ever find the line longer than one person, no customer will turn away, and Bill will bring in just as much money as would Fran. This analysis seems to confirm the original conclusion that Bill would be the better choice.

But there is something about the previous analysis that is bothersome—the excessive use of the word *assume*. Think about it: It is very unlikely that the amount of time between when one customer walks up and when the next customer walks up is exactly the same for all customers. Also, it is very unlikely that the attendant takes *exactly* the same amount of time to make a sno-cone for each customer. Of course, such a sno-cone stand does not exist!

> Modeling the variability between job arrivals and modeling the variability of the job service requirements is crucial.

The truth is that in the real world things do not tend to happen with such predictability. The one customer per minute is an *average*, as is the average number of seconds it takes each attendant to make a sno-cone. Sometimes it takes longer, and sometimes it does not take that long.

It is easy to fall into the trap of thinking that an average is the only kind of characteristic measurement needed when solving problems such as the one involving the sno-cone stand. The amount of time between customer arrivals is really random, with the average of all those random times (if you observed the sno-cone stand for several days) being an average (e.g., one customer every minute). There is a second pitfall: Even knowing that these times are random, people assume that there are just as many "long" times as there are "short" times. That is, they assume that the times are equally distributed about the average. This type of reasoning leads to the assumption that customer arrivals and the time required to make a sno-cone come from a *normal distribution*.

> The normal distribution is also referred to as the Gaussian distribution.

The assumption of a normal distribution of the time between customer arrivals and the time it takes to make sno-cones is also not a wise one. The problem arises when one thinks of *average* and *usual* as being interchangeable words. But the truth is that the *average* time to make a sno-cone is not necessarily the time it *usually* takes to make a sno-cone.

The difference between the *mean* of a distribution and the *median* of a distribution is the issue here. Since times are nonnegative quantities, there is a left boundary (i.e., zero) on the possible values measured. Thus it is often the case that the median is less than the mean. That is, it requires a lot of small numbers to offset a single very large number to maintain the same mean.

Studies have shown that even though the average customer arrival rate is one per minute, the amount of time between customers is usually less than that. It is the occasional lull in business that makes the *average* time between customers seem longer than that which is usually observed. The same is true of the time it takes to make sno-cones. It is those few times when the attendant has to crush more ice, or open a new bottle of cherry flavoring, or engage in any unusual task (e.g., a bathroom break) that tends to slow him or her down that makes the average time to make a sno-cone appear longer than it usually is.

As a further example, consider the list of numbers 1, 2, 3, 2, 12. The average of these numbers is 4, yet if we were to write each number on a slip of paper, mix them up in a hat, and draw one at random, there is a 4 in 5 chance that the number we draw will be less than 4, and only a 1 in 5 chance that the number will be greater than 4.

There is one special distribution, the *exponential distribution*, which does a good job of matching this phenomenon of observed times that are shorter than the average time.

Actually, we should be using the term *negative exponential*, but since most other people use the term *exponential*, so will we.

We will not go into detail about it (you *really* don't want us to!), other than to say that the modeling technique about to be introduced assumes that the time between customer arrivals and the time it takes a person to make a sno-cone are exponentially distributed random values having a known average.

> This is stretching the truth, but it's fine for now. Cynically speaking (with some good underlying mathematical justification), making exponential assumptions is for convenience. It simplifies the analysis and happens to have most of the properties we are looking for.

For the sno-cone-stand problem and all other problems in this book, this is a reasonable assumption.

To make things easier, some new symbols and terms are needed. The amount of time between when one customer comes to the sno-cone stand and when the next customer comes to the sno-cone stand (whether or not the second customer decides to go to Smoothy-Cream) is known as the *interarrival time.* The average time between customers is known as the *mean* interarrival time. (The words *average* and *mean* are interchangeable.)

> The term *mean*, however, is used more frequently.

We can indicate the frequency with which customers arrive at the sno-cone stand either by stating the mean interarrival time or the mean arrival rate (from now on referred to simply as the arrival rate), since one is the inverse of the other. However, it is more common to use the arrival rate, which is denoted by the standard symbol λ.

> By "standard symbol" we mean a notation system generally accepted and understood by the performance evaluation community. The notation used throughout this book is consistent with that used by others.[*]

In our example $\lambda = 1$. That is, customers arrive at the average rate of one customer per minute.

Similarly, we can refer to the *mean service time* and *mean service rate* (simply *service rate*), which are the values associated with how long it takes the

---

[*]P. J. Denning and J. P. Buzen, "The operational analysis of queueing network models," *Computing Surveys* 10, 3(September 1979), 225–261. E. D. Lazowska, J. Zahorjan, G. S. Graham, and K. C. Sevcik, *Quantitative System Performance*, Prentice Hall, Englewood Cliffs, N.J., 1984.

attendant to take care of a customer on average. *Service demand* is synonymous for *service time*. You can think of a customer as "demanding" a certain amount of the attendant's time in order to be serviced. A customer's service demand is denoted by the standard symbol D. In this problem the demand of the customer depends on the attendant. The slower attendant, Bill, takes longer to service customers than does the faster attendant, Fran, meaning that customers will demand more of Bill's time than they will of Fran's. Therefore, every customer demands $D_{\text{Fran}} = \frac{1}{3}$ minute of service if Fran is the attendant and $D_{\text{Bill}} = \frac{1}{2}$ minute of service if Bill is the attendant. However, in the solution technique we are presenting, the service requirement of a customer is often conveniently expressed as a rate. Therefore, we denote the mean service rate by the symbol μ.

> The use of μ, λ, and D causes no problems as long as all customers are statistically identical. Systems in which individual customers have different demands and/or different arrival rates are known as multiclass systems and must be handled more carefully. Multiclass systems are discussed in Chapter 3.

Since rates and times are inverse quantities, $\mu = 1/D$. In our example, $\mu_{\text{Fran}} = 3$ and $\mu_{\text{Bill}} = 2$, meaning that Fran can take care of 3 customers per minute on average, and Bill can take care of 2 customers per minute on average.

The next step is to determine the average number of customers processed each minute, depending on the attendant. This value is known as the *throughput* and is denoted by X. If we can find this value, then the amount of money made each minute will simply be $3X$ dollars. The goal is now to derive an expression for X for each attendant.

At any given time, there can be zero, one, two, or three people at the window. We can think of these as four states of the sno-cone-stand operation, as shown in Figure 1.2. We denote each of these states with a number, which is the same as the number of people in line when the system is in that state. For example, the system is in state 0 when there are no people in line, in state 1 when there is one person in line, and so on. Therefore, all possible states are 0, 1, 2, and 3. Associated with each state i is the probability P_i that if Mr. K were to drive by the stand at a random time (which he does quite often), he would see i people at the window. In other words, there is a P_i probability that

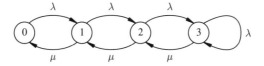

Figure 1.2   State Diagram of the Sno-Cone Stand

the system is in state i. Note that the sum of all the P_i's must be 1, since the system must be in one of the four states at any time. When the sno-cone stand is in state 0, there is no one at the window and the attendant is idle. When the sno-cone stand is in any of the other states, there is at least one person at the window and the attendant is busy (being utilized). Therefore, P_0 is the fraction of time the attendant is idle. The fraction of the time the attendant is not idle is known as the *utilization*, U. Thus $U = 1 - P_0 = P_1 + P_2 + P_3$.

Processor utilization is another performance metric often of interest. The method in which throughput will be calculated depends on knowing the utilization.

Figure 1.2 is a state transition diagram. Such diagrams are helpful in analyzing systems like our sno-cone stand.

The diagram is more formally known as a Markov diagram and its special properties arise from the fact that we have chosen to use the exponential distribution to model service and arrival times. This distribution has a so-called "memoryless" property which makes it easy to work with.

Markov processes are memoryless because, for any state the system can enter, the next state entered depends solely on the current state of the system. States visited previously to the current state and the amount of time spent in the current state or previous states have no bearing on the next transition. This allows time to be factored out of the analysis, which is a BIG help.

At any time, we think of the sno-cone stand as being in exactly one of the four states, which are represented by circles in the diagram. At every "instant" in time, one of two things will happen: Either the state of the sno-cone stand will not change, or the state will change due to the arrival or departure of a customer. For example, if the current state is state 1, the only things that can happen in the next instant of time (aside from nothing happening) are the arrival of a customer (in which case the new state is state 2) or the departure of a customer (in which case the new state is state 0). It is important to realize that at most one "thing" can happen in a single instant of time, and it takes absolutely no time to change state (traverse an arc of the diagram). More specifically, in the very next instant of time, either the state will not change, exactly one customer will arrive, or exactly one customer will depart.

This, too, is a little bit of a lie. Actually, multiple arrivals (or departures) are assumed possible, but only with a *very* small probability that can be ignored. In operating systems, this is okay since systems are driven by a common clock and at most one process is in control of the CPU at any instant.

The possibility of more than one customer arriving or departing simultaneously does not exist since we can think of the amount of time between one "instant" and the next as being as small as necessary to distinguish between the two events. This explains why there is no arc from state 0 to state 2, for example.

The arcs of the diagram are labeled with the rates associated with the change in state they represent. For example, if the current state is state 1, a customer will arrive at rate λ, increasing the length of the line to 2, and the customer currently being served will depart with rate μ, reducing the length of the line to 0. If in state 0, no departures are possible (there is no one at the window), and if in state 3, only a departure will cause a change in state. The arc leaving state 3 that also leads to state 3 represents people who arrive, see three people in line, and go to Smoothy-Cream, leaving the state unchanged.

Suppose that we begin by letting an instant in time be defined as 1 second. This is probably small enough to exclude the possibility of more than one customer arriving or departing in an instant. If, at every instant of time, we were to note the state of the sno-cone stand and compare it with the previous state, we could determine which event occurred to cause a change in state, if any. In other words, we could tell which arc was traversed during the last instant, or determine that no arc was traversed.

The issue being addressed here is that of measurement. Values that serve as input parameters to the model must be obtained in some fashion. In this case, λ, μ_{Bill}, and μ_{Fran} are required. Even though we assumed that Mr. K knew these values a priori, in reality they came from measurement data. Mr. K may have obtained the value for λ by observing other sno-cone stands in the area and counting the number of customer arrivals during some time interval. The rates at which Fran and Bill can fill orders could have been determined by testing them during the job interview (e.g., each was asked to make 100 sno-cones and the average time was determined).

In computer systems, measurements are usually made by a special piece of hardware and/or software called a *monitor*. Monitors vary in sophistication, but usually provide data such as the number of jobs in the system at a given time, and the demands placed on system resources by various jobs.

Since our standard time unit is 1 minute, let's say that at every second we were able to total up the number of times each arc was traversed in the preceding 60 seconds and keep an average of this count for each arc. After we have observed the sno-cone stand for a long time, these averages would tend toward stable values for each arc. We would also be able to calculate the probability of being in a state by calculating the fraction of time spent in that state. These probabilities would also tend toward stable values.

The average number of times an arc is traversed per standard time unit is thought of as the amount of *flow* along that arc. It is obvious that the amount of flow along an arc is heavily dependent on being in the state from which that arc departs. The flow along an arc is simply the product of the probability of being in the state from which the arc departs and the rate associated with the arc. For example, the flow along the arc departing state 0 is λP_0. Remember that after observing the sno-cone stand for a long period of time, these flow values and state probabilities tend to settle down to stable values. This concept is known as *steady state*, meaning that the probability of being in a state is steady over a long period of time. Steady state implies that for any state, the amount of flow into that state must be equal to the amount of flow out of that state. This only makes sense. The analogy of water flowing through pipes between holding basins is valid. If the amount of flow out of a basin were larger than the flow in, conservation of flow would be violated. Over a long period of time all the water would drain out. Steady state would not exist.

This is important stuff! Read it a couple of times.

Remember that the throughput of the attendant is the average number of people that he or she processes in a minute. This is the same as summing the flows of all the arcs that are traversed due to the departure of a customer. In our example, these are all the arcs labeled with μ. To put it another way: total throughput is the sum of the individual state throughputs. The throughput in state 0 is 0, since no one is at the window. The throughput in state 1 is μ, since there is a single customer at the window who departs (i.e., is served) at rate μ. Similarly, the rates at which customers are served in states 2 and 3 are both μ. Taking all of this into consideration, we now have a way to solve for the probabilities of being in each state. Knowing these steady-state probabilities, we can determine the throughput for each attendant by calculating the sum of the flow across the arcs labeled with μ. We know the following:

- Flow along an arc is the product of the probability of being in the state from which the arc departs and the rate associated with that arc.

- The sum of all the flows into a state is equal to the sum of all the flows out of that state.
- The sum over all of the P_i's is 1, since at any time the system must be in one of the four states.
- λ and μ are known values. (λ, the customer arrival rate, is one customer per minute. μ, the service rate, is the inverse of D, which is dependent on the attendant.)

Given these facts, we can write a system of equations that can be solved to yield the steady-state values of the P_i's. For each state in the diagram there is a *balance equation*, which states that the flow into that state is equal to the flow out of that state. The balance equation for state 0 is

$$\mu P_1 = \lambda P_0$$

The left-hand side of the equation is the flow into state 0. Because only one thing can happen at a time, the only way to get into state 0 (i.e., no one at the stand) is to have a customer leave while in state 1. The probability of being in state 1 is P_1 and the rate at which customers leave state 1 is μ. Thus the flow rate into state 0 (from state 1) is μP_1. Similarly, the right-hand side of the equation is the flow out of state 0. It represents a customer arriving at the sno-cone stand when there are no customers. The balance equation for state 1 is

$$\lambda P_0 + \mu P_2 = \lambda P_1 + \mu P_1$$

The left-hand side represents the flow into state 1 and is the sum of arrivals when the system is in state 0 (i.e., λP_0) and departures when the system is in state 2 (i.e., μP_2). The right-hand side represents the flow out of state 1 due to arrivals (i.e., λP_1) and departures (i.e., μP_1).

Each state has a corresponding balance equation. The other balance equations can be written in a similar manner and are given below.

These are the *global balance equations* which yield the steady-state solution.

However, the balance equations by themselves are not enough to solve the system of equations. Even though, in this case, there are four equations in four unknowns (the unknowns are the P_i's—remember that μ and λ are known values), one of the equations is redundant. The fact that all the P_i's sum to 1 provides the additional equation that allows the system to be solved. The entire system of equations for solving the diagram is

$$\mu P_1 = \lambda P_0 \tag{1}$$

$$\lambda P_0 + \mu P_2 = \lambda P_1 + \mu P_1 \tag{2}$$

$$\lambda P_1 + \mu P_3 = \lambda P_2 + \mu P_2 \tag{3}$$

$$\lambda P_2 + \lambda P_3 = \lambda P_3 + \mu P_3 \tag{4}$$

$$P_0 + P_1 + P_2 + P_3 = 1 \tag{5}$$

To see that one of the equations is redundant, consider the following diagram:

The balance equation for state A, flow in = flow out, is $\mu P_B = \lambda P_A$. The balance equation for state B is $\lambda P_A = \mu P_B$. These two equations are identical (i.e., one is redundant).

By using substitution of variables, the system can be solved in terms of P_0 as follows:

$$(1) \implies P_1 = \frac{\lambda}{\mu} P_0 \tag{6}$$

$$(2, 6) \implies P_2 = \frac{\lambda^2}{\mu^2} P_0 \tag{7}$$

$$(3, 6, 7) \implies P_3 = \frac{\lambda^3}{\mu^3} P_0 \tag{8}$$

As you can see, equation (4) is redundant [since it reduces to $P_3 = (\lambda/\mu) P_2 = (\lambda^3/\mu^3) P_0$]. However, given equations (6) to (8) we can state (5) in terms of P_0:

$$P_0 + \frac{\lambda}{\mu} P_0 + \frac{\lambda^2}{\mu^2} P_0 + \frac{\lambda^3}{\mu^3} P_0 = 1$$

which, when rewritten as below, gives the solution to P_0.

$$P_0 = \frac{1}{1 + \lambda/\mu + \lambda^2/\mu^2 + \lambda^3/\mu^3} \qquad (9)$$

Ta da! Given any values for λ and D (from which μ is calculated), (9) will yield the value of P_0, which can then be used in (6) to (8) to yield values for P_1, P_2, and P_3. Table 1.1 shows the final results when the proper values for λ and D are substituted for the cases of Fran and Bill. The steady-state probabilities $P_0 \cdots P_3$ are shown for both individuals.

Other interesting quantities can readily be found once the steady-state probabilities P_0, P_1, P_2, and P_3 are known. For example, the average number of customers at the window is $1 \times P_1 + 2 \times P_2 + 3 \times P_3$ (i.e., 0.45 for Fran and 0.73 for Bill). Also, the rate at which customers leave in a huff for Smoothy-Cream is λP_3 (i.e., 0.025 customer per minute for Fran and 0.067 for Bill).

For example, if Mr. K were to drive by when Fran is working, he would see Fran idle $\frac{27}{40}$ (i.e., 67.5%) of the time and would see three customers at the window $\frac{1}{40}$ (i.e., 2.5%) of the time. Similarly, when Bill is working, he is idle only $\frac{8}{15}$ (i.e., 53.3%) of the time and has 3 customers $\frac{1}{15}$ (i.e., 6.7%) of the time.

Throughput, which is the average number of customers processed per minute, is calculated by summing the amount of flow across arcs labeled with μ. That is, $X = \mu P_1 + \mu P_2 + \mu P_3$. Another way to calculate throughput is as follows. The percentage of time that an attendant is idle (in steady state) is P_0. Thus the percentage of time an attendant is working (i.e., utilization) is $U = 1 - P_0$. While the attendant is working, customers are being pumped out of the system at rate μ. Therefore, if utilization is known and the service demand is known, the throughput of the attendant is given by $X = \mu U = U/D$. This relationship, known as the *utilization law*, is stated as $U = XD$. The utilization law is useful because, given any of the two variables U, X, or D, the third is easily computed. The amount of revenue per minute is simply the product of the throughput for each attendant and the amount of money made per customer, which is \$3. The cost of each employee per minute is subtracted from the revenue gained per minute to yield the profit per minute. These calculations are shown in Table 1.1.

Given these results, we would advise Mr. K to hire Fran instead of Bill since she will bring in a net profit of 3¢ more per minute than Bill. The moral of the story is that first impressions are not always valid and that the assumptions made must be clearly understood since the outcome depends upon them.

TABLE 1.1   Results of Comparison of Fran and Bill

Results	Fran	Bill
λ (arrival rate)	1	1
D (service demand)	1/3	1/2
Steady state probabilities:		
P_0	27/40	8/15
P_1	9/40	4/15
P_2	3/40	2/15
P_3	1/40	1/15
U (utilization)	$1 - P_0$	$1 - P_0$
	$= 1 - 27/40$	$= 1 - 8/15$
	$= 13/40$	$= 7/15$
X (throughput)	U/D	U/D
	$= 13/40 \times 3$	$= 7/15 \times 2$
	$= 39/40$	$= 14/15$
Revenue per minute	$(39/40)(\$3) \approx \$2.93$	$(14/15)(\$3) \approx \$2.80$
Employee cost per minute	\$0.20	\$0.10
Profit per minute	$\$2.93 - \$0.20 = \$2.73$	$\$2.80 - \$0.10 = \$2.70$

1.3 SUMMARY

Table 1.2 gives a brief summary of the notation and important formulas introduced in this section.

TABLE 1.2   Summary

λ	arrival rate
D	service demand
μ	service rate $(\frac{1}{D})$
U	utilization
X	throughput
$U = XD$	utilization law

EXERCISES

1.1 * Bill really wants this job, so he tells Mr. K that he will work for less than \$6
per hour. What pay rate will he have to accept in order to be competitive with
Fran?

1.2 ** Mr. K has interviewed another prospective employee, Bob. Bob has experience
with sno-cones and can complete a transaction in 10 seconds. However, he charges

$18 per hour for his expertise. How much profit does Bob make per minute, and how does he rank with respect to Fran and Bill?

1.3 ** Suppose that Bill improves his service time by 5 seconds. Thus, he completes a transaction in 25 seconds. How does he compare to Fran now?

1.4 **** Assuming that all other problem parameters are as originally stated, what is the minimum amount of time by which Bill must improve his service time in order to be competitive with Fran?

1.5 * Mr. K decides that his price is too high and lowers it. How much will he have to charge per sno-cone in order for Bill and Fran to be competitive? (Note: all other problem parameters are as originally stated.)

1.6 ** Suppose that the customer arrival rate changes to 1 customer every 2 minutes. Which applicant is more profitable, Bill or Fran? By how much?

1.7 **** For what arrival rate is Bill competitive with Fran? What are the ranges of arrival rates for which a) Bill is more cost-effective than Fran; b) Fran is more cost-effective than Bill?

1.8 *** What if the maximum line length changes from 3 to 4? Who is more cost-effective, Fran or Bill? By how much?

1.9 *** Assuming all other parameters are as originally stated, for what range of line lengths will: (a) Bill be more cost-effective; (b) Fran be more cost-effective? Justify your answer.

chapter two

System Design II: Multiple Stations

PROBLEM

JiffyBurger, Inc., is a newly formed corporation that will soon be opening chains of hamburger restaurants across the country. The operation of a typical store is still in the design stages, and corporate officials are trying to finalize the details on how customers will place orders and be served. One decision, however, has been made: Every JiffyBurger will be staffed by exactly two workers at any given time. Exactly how to use them is unresolved.

> In operating systems terminology, this is a multiprocessor system with two CPUs. The best scheduling strategy is at issue.

- Mr. Schnell, the CEO, has suggested that customers get in a single line at the counter, with both attendants working together to fill the order of the first customer in the line.

> This represents a system with very fine grained parallelism (i.e., linear speedup) where two processors can work on a single job simultaneously and complete service in half the time that it would take one processor to do so.

He calls this the *twice-as-fast system*, since two workers can fill an order twice as fast as one working alone.

- Ms. Droll suggests that one worker attend the cash register and the other work the grill. Customers would get into one line at the register where they would place their order and pay, then go to a "Pick Up Order Here" window, where the second worker, after preparing that customer's order, would place it in the window for pickup.

> This models a pipelined system.

She calls this the *sequential system*, since customers go from one line to the next in a sequence.

Other board members believe that the best use of the two workers is to have each of them work both a register and a grill.

> This models more independent, autonomous processors.

First, a worker would take the order, then prepare the food, then accept payment. In this way a customer need only wait in one line, but where this line should be is not clear.

- The second vice-president, Mr. Innis, thinks there should be a separate line for each register, with little rails to keep people from jumping lines. Customers would have a 50:50 chance of getting into either line, he explains, so he calls it the *random-line system*.

- Mrs. Gardener, third vice-president, points out that, in reality, customers are going to choose the shortest line, and calls her system the *shortest-line system*. She agrees with the idea of having rails to keep customers more orderly.
- Freddy the janitor thinks there should be one line in the store and that customers should wait in that line until one of the attendants is free, then step up to that register for full service. He calls this system the *common-line system*.

Given the following, whose solution is best?

- The average time for one worker to perform either job (register or grill) is one minute.
- The average time for 1 worker to perform both jobs is 2 minutes.
- The average time for both workers to perform both jobs for one customer is 1 minute.
- When fewer than three customers are in the store, new customers arrive at an average rate of one every 2 minutes; otherwise, the arrival rate for new customers is zero (i.e., if a customer enters the joint and sees three other customers, he or she will leave immediately and go across the street to NiftyBurger, the competitor).

> The size of the buffer is limited to three, meaning that the arrival process "cuts off" when the buffer is full. In this problem, the customers *balk*, meaning that they see the buffer is full and go to NiftyBurger. In some systems, a full buffer causes the source of the customers to be *blocked* (i.e., turned off) until the buffer becomes nonfull. You can think of this as customers staying at home until the buffer becomes nonfull.

In order to answer this question, Mr. Schnell has hired you to study the different proposals and make recommendations.

2.1 APPLICATION TO OPERATING SYSTEMS

Consider a situation in which a new computer is being designed. The designer has the choice of building the computer using a single processor, or using two processors, each half as fast as the single processor. This problem explores several possible designs. The design incorporating the single processor is analogous to the twice-as-fast system that Mr. Schnell suggested. Ms. Droll's suggestion is equivalent to using two slower processors in series (e.g., a job uses one processor for calculation and another for I/O). The other three suggestions propose using two slower processors in parallel; the way in which jobs are assigned to processors is varied.

The designer of the system will wish it to perform optimally with respect to some *objective function*. For example, if the designer wants the system to process the most jobs in the shortest amount of time, the objective function is to maximize throughput. However, if the designer wishes jobs to wait the shortest amount of time before receiving service, the objective function is to minimize wait time. The objective function depends on the application, and the choice of design is that which best satisfies the objective function.

2.2 SOLVING THE ALTERNATIVE MODELS

Each board member has proposed a system for managing customers in the store. Before comparing the board members' systems, we must make a model of each for study. We assume exponentially distributed service and arrival times since:

1. Neither Mr. Schnell nor the board specified what additional assumptions should be made.
2. Due to the discussion of the previous problem, exponential assumptions are reasonable.
3. It makes life much easier (i.e., making other assumptions would *really* complicate the analysis while adding no additional insight into the problem).

With these assumptions, we can use the state diagram and balance equations we learned in the preceding chapter to analyze each system. From our analysis we can determine the utilization U of each server and, using the utilization law introduced in Chapter 1, we can compute throughput X. If we let 1 minute be our standard unit of time, then for every alternative model the following information is the same:

- The mean customer arrival rate, $\lambda = \frac{1}{2}$.
- The maximum capacity is three customers.
- The time it takes one person to do either job, $D_e = 1/\mu_e = 1$.
- The time it takes one person to do both jobs, $D_b = 1/\mu_b = 2$.
- The time it takes two people to do both jobs together, $D_t = 1/\mu_t = 1$.

2.2.1 Twice-As-Fast System

Mr. Schnell wants both workers to serve a single customer at the same time—called the *twice-as-fast system*. Let us refer to this as system TAF. Together, both workers serve the customer at the head of the line with mean rate $\mu_t = 1$. Figure 2.1(a) illustrates how customers move through the restaurant. Customers enter from the left side of the diagram in the direction of the arrow. They then get into a line where they wait for service. The customer at the head of the line receives service from the two workers working together. Service is received at rate μ_t. After service is received, the customer exits, as indicated by the arrow.

The state diagram for system TAF, shown in Figure 2.1(b), is exactly the same as the diagram of the sno-cone stand in Chapter 1.

The self-looping arc from state 3 to state 3 is not needed in either problem. It was included in the previous problem for completeness. Inspection of the balance equations will reveal why the arc is unimportant—a common term can be deleted from both sides of the equation.

Therefore, the same balance equations apply to system TAF.

$$\lambda P_0 = \mu_t P_1$$
$$(\lambda + \mu_t)P_1 = \lambda P_0 + \mu_t P_2$$
$$(\lambda + \mu_t)P_2 = \lambda P_1 + \mu_t P_3$$
$$\mu_t P_3 = \lambda P_2$$
$$\sum P_i = 1$$

Solving the system of equations yields

$$P_0 = \frac{\mu_t^3}{\lambda^3 + \lambda^2 \mu_t + \lambda \mu_t^2 + \mu_t^3}$$

$$P_1 = \frac{\lambda \mu_t^2}{\lambda^3 + \lambda^2 \mu_t + \lambda \mu_t^2 + \mu_t^3}$$

$$P_2 = \frac{\lambda^2 \mu_t}{\lambda^3 + \lambda^2 \mu_t + \lambda \mu_t^2 + \mu_t^3}$$

$$P_3 = \frac{\lambda^3}{\lambda^3 + \lambda^2 \mu_t + \lambda \mu_t^2 + \mu_t^3}$$

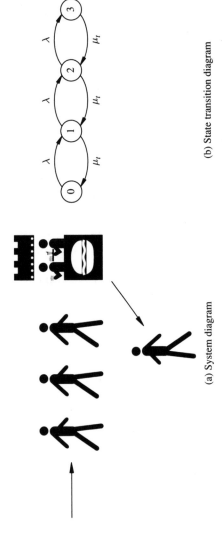

(a) System diagram

(b) State transition diagram

Figure 2.1 Diagrams for system TAF (twice as fast)

Substituting $\lambda = \frac{1}{2}$ and $\mu_t = 1$, we can find the steady-state probabilities of being in any state of the system.

$$P_0 = \frac{8}{15}$$

$$P_1 = \frac{4}{15}$$

$$P_2 = \frac{2}{15}$$

$$P_3 = \frac{1}{15}$$

We are considering this system to be a single server comprised of two workers. The utilization of the server is given by $1 - P_0$, where P_0 is the probability that the server is idle. Therefore, utilization of the server is

$$U_{\text{TAF}} = 1 - P_0$$

$$= 1 - \frac{8}{15}$$

$$= \frac{7}{15}$$

This means that $\frac{7}{15}$ of the time, the twice-as-fast server has something to do. Now, using the utilization law, $U = XD$, we can find the throughput of system TAF as follows:

$$X_{\text{TAF}} = \frac{U_{\text{TAF}}}{D_t}$$

$$= \frac{7/15}{1}$$

$$= \frac{7}{15}$$

2.2.2 Sequential System

Ms. Droll has suggested the use of two lines, as shown in Figure 2.2(a). Customers will first place their orders at one line, then wait in another line for their orders to be filled. We call this system SEQ since the two lines are visited sequentially by customers. The state diagram for system SEQ is a little more complicated than for system TAF and is shown in Figure 2.2(b). The state of

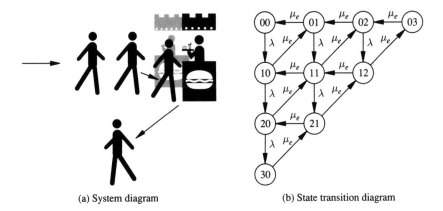

(a) System diagram   (b) State transition diagram

Figure 2.2   Diagrams for system SEQ (sequential)

the system can no longer be expressed as the length of a single line in the restaurant. Instead, the state depends on the length of both the lines. Let ij indicate a state in which there are i people in the first line placing orders and j people in the second line picking up orders. There are 10 possible states: 00, 01, 02, 03, 10, 11, 12, 20, 21, and 30.

Customers entering the store at rate λ must first be served at the first line, where they place their order and pay at rate μ_e. After finishing at the first line, customers move to the second line, where they pick up their order, and then leave the store at rate μ_e. The system of balance equations that comes from the diagram is

$$\lambda P_{00} = \mu_e P_{01}$$

$$(\lambda + \mu_e) P_{01} = \mu_e P_{02} + \mu_e P_{10}$$

$$(\lambda + \mu_e) P_{02} = \mu_e P_{03} + \mu_e P_{11}$$

$$\mu_e P_{03} = \mu_e P_{12}$$

$$(\lambda + \mu_e) P_{10} = \lambda P_{00} + \mu_e P_{11}$$

$$(\lambda + 2\mu_e) P_{11} = \lambda P_{01} + \mu_e P_{12} + \mu_e P_{20}$$

$$2\mu_e P_{12} = \lambda P_{02} + \mu_e P_{21}$$

$$(\lambda + \mu_e) P_{20} = \lambda P_{10} + \mu_e P_{21}$$

$$2\mu_e P_{21} = \lambda P_{11} + \mu_e P_{30}$$

$$\mu_e P_{30} = \lambda P_{20}$$

$$\sum P_{ij} = 1$$

As before, one of the first 10 equations is redundant. The solution to these balance equations is

$$P_{00} = \frac{\mu_e^3}{4\lambda^3 + 3\lambda^2\mu_e + 2\lambda\mu_e^2 + \mu_e^3}$$

$$P_{01} = P_{10} = \frac{\lambda\mu_e^2}{4\lambda^3 + 3\lambda^2\mu_e + 2\lambda\mu_e^2 + \mu_e^3}$$

$$P_{02} = P_{11} = P_{20} = \frac{\lambda^2\mu_e}{4\lambda^3 + 3\lambda^2\mu_e + 2\lambda\mu_e^2 + \mu_e^3}$$

$$P_{03} = P_{12} = P_{21} = P_{30} = \frac{\lambda^3}{4\lambda^3 + 3\lambda^2\mu_e + 2\lambda\mu_e^2 + \mu_e^3}$$

We notice that many states have the same solution: $P_{10} = P_{01}$, $P_{20} = P_{11} = P_{02}$ and $P_{30} = P_{21} = P_{12} = P_{03}$. Identifying these sets of equivalent states in the diagram, we discover that for each set, the states fall on the same diagonal line. This kind of symmetry is typical. Failure to find the symmetry in a solution is often good reason to recheck one's work. This is not to say, however, that all systems display such symmetry.

Finally, substituting values for $\lambda = \frac{1}{2}$ and $\mu_e = 1$, the steady-state probabilities for this particular system are

$$P_{00} = \frac{4}{13}$$

$$P_{10} = P_{01} = \frac{2}{13}$$

$$P_{20} = P_{11} = P_{02} = \frac{1}{13}$$

$$P_{30} = P_{21} = P_{12} = P_{03} = \frac{1}{26}$$

Again, we use the utilization law, $U = XD$, to determine the throughput of this system. There are two servers in this system, though. Do we use the utilization and demand of the first server, the second server, or somehow "average" them together?

The answer comes by looking at the *topology* of the system, meaning the connections between the servers. The topology of system SEQ is a straight line: customers (A) enter the restaurant, (B) are served by the first server (place order), (C) are served by the second server (pick up order), and (D) exit the store. This sequence of events is shown in Figure 2.3. Remember that we have assumed that our system is in steady-state. A consequence of this assumption is that, for any state, flow into that state is equal to flow out of that state. A generalization of this concept is that flow into the system must be equal to flow out of the system. Since the topology of this system is strictly sequential, we

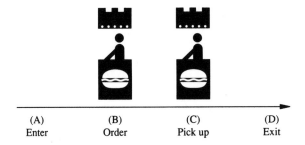

| (A) | (B) | (C) | (D) |
| Enter | Order | Pick up | Exit |

Figure 2.3 Topology of system SEQ

can measure throughput at any point along the line shown in the figure and it will be the same. We know the utilizations and demands for points B and C, so either of these points will do. Let us consider point B, which is the first server.

Utilization of the first server, U_{SEQ1}, can be obtained by summing the probabilities of all states in which there are no customers at the first server (idle time), and subtracting this sum from 1. Any state that has a zero as the first digit of its label is included in the summation.

$$U_{\text{SEQ1}} = 1 - (P_{00} + P_{01} + P_{02} + P_{03})$$
$$= 1 - \frac{4}{13} - \frac{2}{13} - \frac{1}{13} - \frac{1}{26}$$
$$= \frac{11}{26}$$

Demand at the first server is D_e, which is 1. Therefore, throughput of the first server is given by

$$X_{\text{SEQ1}} = \frac{U_{\text{SEQ1}}}{D_e}$$
$$= \frac{11}{26}$$

which is the throughput of the system. Let us compute throughput at point C to verify that it will be the same. Utilization of the second server, U_{SEQ2}, is obtained by summing the probabilities of all states having a zero as the second digit in the state label and subtracting this sum from 1.

$$U_{\text{SEQ2}} = 1 - (P_{00} + P_{10} + P_{20} + P_{30})$$
$$= 1 - \frac{4}{13} - \frac{2}{13} - \frac{1}{13} - \frac{1}{26}$$
$$= \frac{11}{26}$$

Demand at the second server is also D_e, which is 1. Therefore, throughput of the second server is

$$X_{SEQ2} = \frac{U_{SEQ2}}{D_e}$$

$$= \frac{11}{26}$$

which is the same as X_{SEQ1}.

2.2.3 Random-Line System

Mr. Innis described a system in which there are two full-service lines, each served by a single worker, as shown in Figure 2.4(a). Customers enter the store and randomly choose a line; therefore, we will refer to this system as system RL. We shall interpret the word *random* to mean that the probability of choosing a line is the same for all lines. Since there are two lines in this system, then the probability of choosing any particular line is $\frac{1}{2}$. Therefore, customers entering the store arrive at either line with rate $\lambda/2$. Each line is full-service in the sense that customers place their orders and pick them up in the same line at rate μ_b.

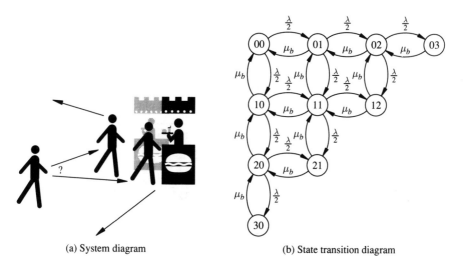

(a) System diagram   (b) State transition diagram

Figure 2.4   Diagrams for system RL (random line)

The state diagram for system RL is shown in Figure 2.4(b). Notice that the system has the same set of states as system SEQ, but the transitions between states are quite different. The system of balance equations for system RL is

$$\lambda P_{00} = \mu_b P_{01} + \mu_b P_{10}$$

$$(\lambda + \mu_b) P_{01} = \frac{\lambda}{2} P_{00} + \mu_b P_{02} + \mu_b P_{11}$$

$$(\lambda + \mu_b) P_{02} = \frac{\lambda}{2} P_{01} + \mu_b P_{03} + \mu_b P_{12}$$

$$\mu_b P_{03} = \frac{\lambda}{2} P_{02}$$

$$(\lambda + \mu_b) P_{10} = \frac{\lambda}{2} P_{00} + \mu_b P_{11} + \mu_b P_{20}$$

$$(\lambda + 2\mu_b) P_{11} = \frac{\lambda}{2} P_{01} + \frac{\lambda}{2} P_{10} + \mu_b P_{12} + \mu_b P_{21}$$

$$2\mu_b P_{12} = \frac{\lambda}{2} P_{02} + \frac{\lambda}{2} P_{11}$$

$$(\lambda + \mu_b) P_{20} = \frac{\lambda}{2} P_{10} + \mu_b P_{30} + \mu_b P_{21}$$

$$2\mu_b P_{21} = \frac{\lambda}{2} P_{20} + \frac{\lambda}{2} P_{11}$$

$$\mu_b P_{30} = \frac{\lambda}{2} P_{20}$$

$$\sum P_{ij} = 1$$

All these equations "look" bad but are not difficult. First, study the state diagram and verify its correctness. Then these equations can be written directly from the diagram.

The steady-state solution for system RL is

$$P_{00} = \frac{4\mu_b^3}{2\lambda^3 + 3\lambda^2 \mu_b + 4\lambda \mu_b^2 + 4\mu_b^3}$$

$$P_{01} = P_{10} = \frac{2\lambda \mu_b^2}{2\lambda^3 + 3\lambda^2 \mu_b + 4\lambda \mu_b^2 + 4\mu_b^3}$$

$$P_{02} = P_{11} = P_{20} = \frac{\lambda^2 \mu_b}{2\lambda^3 + 3\lambda^2 \mu_b + 4\lambda \mu_b^2 + 4\mu_b^3}$$

$$P_{03} = P_{12} = P_{21} = P_{30} = \frac{\frac{\lambda^3}{2}}{2\lambda^3 + 3\lambda^2 \mu_b + 4\lambda \mu_b^2 + 4\mu_b^3}$$

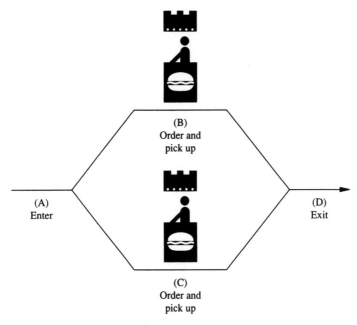

Figure 2.5 Topology of system RL

Substituting $\lambda = \frac{1}{2}$ and $\mu_b = \frac{1}{2}$ the steady-state probabilities for system RL are

$$P_{00} = \frac{4}{13}$$

$$P_{01} = P_{10} = \frac{2}{13}$$

$$P_{02} = P_{11} = P_{20} = \frac{1}{13}$$

$$P_{03} = P_{12} = P_{21} = P_{30} = \frac{1}{26}$$

This is the same solution as for system SEQ, but are the throughputs of the two systems also the same?

To find the throughput of system RL we must again consider the system topology, which is shown in Figure 2.5. Every customer will take either path (A,B,D) or (A,C,D) through the system. Therefore, to get the throughput of the system we must measure throughput at both points B and C, the two servers, and add them together.

$$U_{RL1} = 1 - (P_{00} + P_{01} + P_{02} + P_{03})$$

$$= 1 - \frac{4}{13} - \frac{2}{13} - \frac{1}{13} - \frac{1}{26}$$

$$= \frac{11}{26}$$

$$U_{RL2} = 1 - (P_{00} + P_{10} + P_{20} + P_{30})$$

$$= 1 - \frac{4}{13} - \frac{2}{13} - \frac{1}{13} - \frac{1}{26}$$

$$= \frac{11}{26}$$

$$X_{RL} = X_{RL1} + X_{RL2}$$

$$= \frac{U_{RL1}}{D_b} + \frac{U_{RL2}}{D_b}$$

$$= \frac{11/26}{2} + \frac{11/26}{2}$$

$$= \frac{11}{26}$$

We see that the throughputs of system SEQ and system RL are the same.

2.2.4 Shortest Line System

Mrs. Gardener pointed out to Mr. Innis and the rest of the board that customers are more likely to choose the shortest line to get into when they enter the restaurant. Her system is exactly like Mr. Innis's except that when lengths of the two lines are different, an arriving customer will get into the shorter line, as shown in Figure 2.6(a). When the line lengths are the same, there is an equal probability of a customer getting into any particular line. The state diagram for

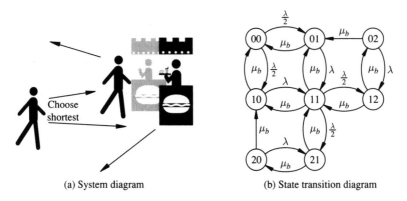

(a) System diagram (b) State transition diagram

Figure 2.6 Diagrams for system SL (shortest line)

this system, which we will refer to as system SL, is given in Figure 2.6(b). The system of balance equations is

$$\lambda P_{00} = \mu_b P_{01} + \mu_b P_{10}$$

$$(\lambda + \mu_b) P_{01} = \frac{\lambda}{2} P_{00} + \mu_b P_{02} + \mu_b P_{11}$$

$$(\lambda + \mu_b) P_{02} = \mu_b P_{12}$$

$$(\lambda + \mu_b) P_{10} = \frac{\lambda}{2} P_{00} + \mu_b P_{20} + \mu_b P_{11}$$

$$(\lambda + 2\mu_b) P_{11} = \lambda P_{01} + \lambda P_{10} + \mu_b P_{12} + \mu_b P_{21}$$

$$2\mu_b P_{12} = \lambda P_{02} + \frac{\lambda}{2} P_{11}$$

$$(\lambda + \mu_b) P_{20} = \mu_b P_{21}$$

$$2\mu_b P_{21} = \frac{\lambda}{2} P_{11} + \lambda P_{20}$$

$$\sum P_{ij} = 1$$

The solution set is

$$P_{00} = \frac{\mu_b^3(3\lambda + 4\mu_b)}{\lambda^4 + 3\lambda^3\mu_b + 5\lambda^2\mu_b^2 + 7\lambda\mu_b^3 + 4\mu_b^4}$$

$$P_{01} = P_{10} = \frac{[\lambda\mu_b^2(3\lambda + 4\mu_b)]/2}{\lambda^4 + 3\lambda^3\mu_b + 5\lambda^2\mu_b^2 + 7\lambda\mu_b^3 + 4\mu_b^4}$$

$$P_{02} = P_{20} = \frac{\lambda^3\mu_b/2}{\lambda^4 + 3\lambda^3\mu_b + 5\lambda^2\mu_b^2 + 7\lambda\mu_b^3 + 4\mu_b^4}$$

$$P_{11} = \frac{\lambda^2\mu_b(\lambda + 2\mu_b)}{\lambda^4 + 3\lambda^3\mu_b + 5\lambda^2\mu_b^2 + 7\lambda\mu_b^3 + 4\mu_b^4}$$

$$P_{12} = P_{21} = \frac{[\lambda^3(\lambda + \mu_b)]/2}{\lambda^4 + 3\lambda^3\mu_b + 5\lambda^2\mu_b^2 + 7\lambda\mu_b^3 + 4\mu_b^4}$$

With $\lambda = \frac{1}{2}$ and $\mu_b = \frac{1}{2}$, the steady-state probabilities for system SL are:

$$P_{00} = \frac{7}{20}$$

$$P_{01} = P_{10} = \frac{7}{40}$$

$$P_{02} = P_{20} = \frac{1}{40}$$

$$P_{11} = \frac{3}{20}$$

$$P_{12} = P_{21} = \frac{1}{20}$$

Since the topology of system SL is the same as system RL (see Figure 2.5), throughput is found in the same way. That is, we find the throughputs of the two servers and add them together.

$$U_{SL1} = 1 - (P_{00} + P_{01} + P_{02})$$

$$= 1 - \frac{7}{20} - \frac{7}{40} - \frac{1}{40}$$

$$= \frac{9}{20}$$

$$U_{SL2} = 1 - (P_{00} + P_{10} + P_{20})$$

$$= 1 - \frac{7}{20} - \frac{7}{40} - \frac{1}{40}$$

$$= \frac{9}{20}$$

$$X_{SL} = X_{SL1} + X_{SL2}$$

$$= \frac{U_{SL1}}{D_b} + \frac{U_{SL2}}{D_b}$$

$$= \frac{9/20}{2} + \frac{9/20}{2}$$

$$= \frac{9}{20}$$

2.2.5 Common-Line System

Freddy, who often sits in on board meetings, suggested a system that is popular in banks and post offices. In this system, shown in Figure 2.7(a), there is one long line where everyone waits. When a worker becomes free, the person at the head of the line goes to that worker to be served. All the workers draw customers from a common, shared line, which is why Freddy calls this the common-line system. We will refer to it as system CL.

Figure 2.7(b) shows the state diagram for this system. The state description in this diagram is slightly different from the previous three. Each state is marked

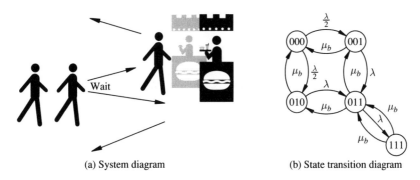

(a) System diagram   (b) State transition diagram

Figure 2.7   Diagrams for system CL (common line)

with three numbers, for example, ijk, where i is the number of people waiting in the common line, j is 1 or 0 depending on whether or not the first worker is busy serving a customer, and k (like j) is 1 or 0 depending on whether the second worker is busy serving a customer. The balance equations for system CL are

$$\lambda P_{000} = \mu_b P_{001} + \mu_b P_{010}$$

$$(\lambda + \mu_b) P_{001} = \frac{\lambda}{2} P_{000} + \mu_b P_{011}$$

$$(\lambda + \mu_b) P_{010} = \frac{\lambda}{2} P_{000} + \mu_b P_{011}$$

$$(\lambda + 2\mu_b) P_{011} = \lambda P_{001} + \lambda P_{010} + 2\mu_b P_{111}$$

$$2\mu_b P_{111} = \lambda P_{011}$$

$$\sum P_{ijk} = 1$$

The steady-state solution is

$$P_{000} = \frac{4\mu_b^3}{\lambda^3 + 2\lambda^2 \mu_b + 4\lambda \mu_b^2 + 4\mu_b^3}$$

$$P_{001} = P_{010} = \frac{2\lambda \mu_b^2}{\lambda^3 + 2\lambda^2 \mu_b + 4\lambda \mu_b^2 + 4\mu_b^3}$$

$$P_{011} = \frac{2\lambda^2 \mu_b}{\lambda^3 + 2\lambda^2 \mu_b + 4\lambda \mu_b^2 + 4\mu_b^3}$$

$$P_{111} = \frac{\lambda^3}{\lambda^3 + 2\lambda^2 \mu_b + 4\lambda \mu_b^2 + 4\mu_b^3}$$

With $\lambda = \frac{1}{2}$ and $\mu_b = \frac{1}{2}$, the steady state probabilities for system CL are:

$$P_{000} = \frac{4}{11}$$

$$P_{001} = P_{010} = P_{011} = \frac{2}{11}$$

$$P_{111} = \frac{1}{11}$$

Throughput of system CL is

$$U_{CL1} = 1 - (P_{000} + P_{001})$$

$$= 1 - \frac{4}{11} - \frac{2}{11}$$

$$= \frac{5}{11}$$

$$U_{CL2} = 1 - (P_{000} + P_{010})$$

$$= 1 - \frac{4}{11} - \frac{2}{11}$$

$$= \frac{5}{11}$$

$$X_{CL} = X_{CL1} + X_{CL2}$$

$$= \frac{U_{CL1}}{D_b} + \frac{U_{CL2}}{D_b}$$

$$= \frac{5/11}{2} + \frac{5/11}{2}$$

$$= \frac{5}{11}$$

2.3 COMPARING THE ALTERNATIVES

Now that we have solved for the steady-state probabilities for each of the proposed alternatives, we can compare them to see which is best. But what do we mean by *best*? That is, what is the most appropriate objective function to use in determining a ranking of systems with respect to desirability? In the preceding problem, the best worker was hired depending on the throughput of the sno-cone stand when he or she worked. We can apply a similar notion of *best* to the JiffyBurger problem. That is, the system that has the highest throughput is the best. The highest throughput will mean the most customers being served per minute, hence more money made.

But there are other measures of *best* that should also be considered. Suppose that a system has high throughput, but customers spend a lot of time in the restaurant. Over time, customers may not like coming to JiffyBurger because it takes too long to get in and out. Thus, as a function of time, λ may decrease due to dissatisfied customers. The length of time between entering the restaurant and leaving it is known as the *response time* of the system. It is the average amount of time a customer spends in the restaurant. Hence, another objective function would be to minimize the response time. This will undoubtedly please the customers, which may result in an increased arrival rate λ.

Another way to rank systems would be to compare *wait times*, that is, the amount of time a customer must wait while not receiving service. Customers do not seem to mind standing in line as long as they know they are being waited on. Wait time is simply the response time of the system less the average service time.

So now we have three different objective functions by which to rank these five systems. Instead of deciding which of these is the proper "best" criterion, we will find all three rankings, present them to the board, and let them decide which is most appropriate.

Other objective functions are feasible. Examples include minimizing server idle time, minimizing the number of customers who go to NiftyBurger, minimizing the variance between customer response times, and so on. The proper objective function is always a management decision.

2.3.1 Ranking by Throughput

Table 2.1 shows the throughputs of each system. We see that system TAF is the best (having the highest throughput), followed by system CL, system SL, system RL, and system SEQ. Intuitively, this makes sense. The best throughput is achieved when all of the server "power" is concentrated in one place. Whenever there is anyone in the restaurant, the server (both workers working together) is utilized. The other schemes, however, allow for a worker to be idle while the restaurant is not empty.

System CL has better throughput than system SL, but is the difference really significant? A look at the percentage improvement of one system over another shows that system CL delivers only 0.8% more throughput than system SL. Comparing system CL to system SEQ shows an improvement of 7.3%.

TABLE 2.1
Throughputs of
Proposed JiffyBurger
Systems

X_{TAF}	=	0.466
X_{SEQ}	=	0.423
X_{RL}	=	0.423
X_{SL}	=	0.450
X_{CL}	=	0.454

Similarly, system SL is 6.3% better than system SEQ. Many other comparisons could be made. The choice between system CL and system SL may be affected by other considerations, since the two systems are so "close" when throughputs are compared.

2.3.2 Ranking by Response Time

A special relationship that we will make use of in calculating response time is known as *Little's result** (or *Little's law*):

$$N = XR$$

N is the average number of people in line, X is the average throughput, and R is the average time that a customer stays in the line. As we shall see, R is the response time (also called "residence time"). Little's result is straightforward and intuitive. It says that if we were to watch the line for a period of time R, we would see N customers get into the line (on the average). Or, viewed differently, every R time units (i.e., the average amount of time it takes a customer to pass through the line) N customers will leave the line and N customers will arrive and get into the line.

Rewriting Little's result, we obtain

$$R = \frac{N}{X}$$

This implies that if we know the throughput and the average number of customers in the line, we can find the average elapsed time between a customer's arrival and its departure. These facts are easy to see, but applying them to finding response time requires a "little" thought.

Consider a piece of pipe that is eight times as long as the width of a Ping-Pong ball. If we were to force a Ping-Pong ball into one end of the pipe on the average of two per minute, we would expect a particular Ping-Pong ball to take 4 minutes to pop out the other end of the pipe once the pipe was filled. In this example, $N = 8$, $X = 2$, and $R = N/X = 4$.

*J. D. C. Little, "A proof of the queueing formula $L = \lambda W$," *Operations Research* 9, 3 (1961), 383–387.

This relationship holds even if we allow the balls to be shuffled within the pipe since we are considering *average* values.

Let us now apply Little's result to the JiffyBurger problem. We have already calculated X for each of the systems under consideration. The only other quantity we need is N, the average line length (i.e., the average number of customers in the restaurant).

Knowing steady-state probabilities for each system state allows us to calculate N. For each state we can determine the number of customers in the restaurant when the system is in that state and weight it with the steady-state probability of being in that state. Summing these values over every state will yield the average number of customers in the system in steady state (i.e., N). That is, if there are $n(x)$ customers when the system is in state x, then $N = \sum n(x) P_x$ for all x (i.e., for all states).

Knowing N and X, we can find the response time R for each system. It does not matter what the inside of the restaurant looks like (i.e., which of the five systems we are using) as long as we know the average throughput and the average number of people in the restaurant. Table 2.2 shows these calculations for each system.

These results indicate that with respect to response time, the best system is system TAF, then system CL, system SL, system RL, and system SEQ (the last two being equivalent). It is interesting to note that this is the same ranking as that obtained when the systems were compared based on throughput.

Often, ranking by throughput and ranking by response time are opposing objectives. Throughput is often maximized by keeping the system as highly utilized as possible. Response time is minimized with low system utilization so that when a customer arrives, the customer doesn't spend time waiting to be served. However, by viewing Little's result, if N were a fixed constant, minimizing R would maximize X. This is an apparent paradox. Without going into detail here, the following rule of thumb applies: If there is an upper limit on the number of customers allowed (i.e., a *closed system*), as in this example, then maximizing throughput and minimizing response time are complementary. If no limit on the number of customers exists (i.e., an *open system*), these are conflicting objectives.

2.3.3 Ranking by Wait Time

Wait time, W, is the amount of time a customer spends waiting but not receiving service. It can be calculated by subtracting the average service time

TABLE 2.2   Response Times of Proposed JiffyBurger Systems

$$R_{TAF} = \frac{N_{TAF}}{X_{TAF}}$$

$$= \frac{0P_0 + 1P_1 + 2P_2 + 3P_3}{X_{TAF}}$$

$$= \frac{0(8/15) + 1(4/15) + 2(2/15) + 3(1/15)}{0.466}$$

$$= 1.571$$

$$R_{SEQ} = \frac{N_{SEQ}}{X_{SEQ}}$$

$$= \frac{0P_{00} + 1(P_{01} + P_{10}) + 2(P_{20} + P_{11} + P_{02}) + 3(P_{30} + P_{21} + P_{12} + P_{03})}{X_{SEQ}}$$

$$= \frac{0(4/13) + 1(2/13 + 2/13) + 2(1/13 + 1/13 + 1/13) + 3(1/26 + 1/26 + 1/26 + 1/26)}{0.423}$$

$$= 2.909$$

$$R_{RL} = \frac{N_{RL}}{X_{RL}}$$

$$= \frac{0P_{00} + 1(P_{01} + P_{10}) + 2(P_{20} + P_{11} + P_{02}) + 3(P_{30} + P_{21} + P_{12} + P_{03})}{X_{RL}}$$

$$= \frac{0(4/13) + 1(2/13 + 2/13) + 2(1/13 + 1/13 + 1/13) + 3(1/26 + 1/26 + 1/26 + 1/26)}{0.423}$$

$$= 2.909$$

$$R_{SL} = \frac{N_{SL}}{X_{SL}}$$

$$= \frac{0P_{00} + 1(P_{01} + P_{10}) + 2(P_{20} + P_{11} + P_{02}) + 3(P_{21} + P_{12})}{X_{SL}}$$

$$= \frac{0(7/20) + 1(7/40 + 7/40) + 2(1/40 + 3/20 + 1/40) + 3(1/20 + 1/20)}{0.450}$$

$$= 2.333$$

$$R_{CL} = \frac{N_{CL}}{X_{CL}}$$

$$= \frac{0P_{000} + 1(P_{001} + P_{010}) + 2P_{011} + 3P_{111}}{X_{CL}}$$

$$= \frac{0(4/11) + 1(2/11 + 2/11) + 2(2/11) + 3(1/11)}{0.454}$$

$$= 2.202$$

from the average response time. For system SEQ, the average service time for the entire restaurant is the sum of the individual service times at the register and grill. Table 2.3 shows the calculation of the average wait time for each system.

These results rank the systems as system CL being the best, followed by system SL, system TAF, system RL and system SEQ (the latter two being equivalent). With respect to the other two rankings, the top three contenders exchange places. System TAF, which has the highest throughput and shortest response time, has a longer wait time than system CL and system SL.

TABLE 2.3 Wait Times
of Proposed JiffyBurger
Systems

W_{TAF}	$= R_{TAF} - D_t$
	$= 1.571 - 1$
	$= 0.571$
W_{SEQ}	$= R_{SEQ} - 2D_e$
	$= 2.909 - 2$
	$= 0.909$
W_{RL}	$= R_{RL} - D_b$
	$= 2.909 - 2$
	$= 0.909$
W_{SL}	$= R_{SL} - D_b$
	$= 2.333 - 2$
	$= 0.333$
W_{CL}	$= R_{CL} - D_b$
	$= 2.202 - 2$
	$= 0.202$

2.4 RECOMMENDATIONS TO THE BOARD

Given the rankings of systems, our report to the JiffyBurger board would be as follows.

The sequential and random-line systems are identical in all three rankings. Furthermore, they are the worst schemes in all rankings and should not be considered. Because throughputs of the shortest and common-line systems are so close, there is no advantage in choosing shortest over common, especially since the common line has a faster response time.

So the choice comes down to either the twice-as-fast system or the common-line system. For maximum throughput, the twice-as-fast system should be chosen. It gives 8% higher throughput. For minimum wait time, the common-line system should be chosen. It gives 58% less waiting time. (However, remember that this excludes service time. With service time included, system TAF is better by 33% as seen by comparing overall response times.) The board can choose to maximize throughput, which means more money made, or the board can choose to minimize wait time, which <u>may</u> mean happier customers. We must remind the board that happier customers may mean an increased customer arrival rate in the future (which means higher throughput, eventually) but that less money will be made initially. On the other hand, maximizing throughput will now mean more money immediately, but perhaps customers, disgruntled with the longer wait time (twice as long as for the common-line system), will stop coming to JiffyBurger, which decreases the customer arrival rate in the future (resulting in decreased throughput). However, based solely on throughput and overall response time, we recommend using the twice-as-fast system. (The CEO often has good insight, but the janitor is usually not far behind!)

We would *strongly* emphasize that other factors should be considered by the board. One factor that may affect the board's decision is *reliability*, also known as *fault tolerance*. The common-line system is more reliable than the twice-as-fast system. If the cash register of the twice-as-fast system breaks, the restaurant is not capable of serving any customers. However, if one of the cash registers of the common-line system breaks, the other one is still usable and the restaurant can continue to serve customers (although throughput and response time will be diminished). Another factor is job specialization. In the twice-as-fast system, each worker is trained for one specialty. The job training time may be shorter but if a worker calls in sick, a replacement will probably not be as efficient. In the common-line system each worker is trained to do all jobs. Job training takes longer, but the system performance is more stable since all workers know all jobs.

2.5 SUMMARY

Table 2.4 gives a brief summary of the notation and important formulas introduced in this chapter.

TABLE 2.4   Section Summary

R	response time
W	wait time
$N = XR$	Little's law

EXERCISES

2.1 ** Reconsider system RL. Let the demand at one of the servers be one half that of the other server. What will the ratio of server utilizations be? Solve the steady-state equations to verify your answer.

2.2 *** Give an intuitive explanation of why system RL and system SEQ have the same throughput by answering the following questions. a) Do RL and SEQ always have the same throughput, even for different values of D_e and D_b if the constraint $D_b = 2D_e$ is imposed? b) Suppose that the demands on the two servers in the system SEQ are D_1 and D_2 and that the demands on the two servers in system RL are D_3 and D_4. If the constraint $D_1 + D_2 = D_3 + D_4$ is imposed, are the throughputs of system SEQ and system RL identical for all values of D_1, D_2, D_3, and D_4?

2.3 ** Suppose that the time it takes two people to do both jobs together is $D_t = \frac{1}{\mu_t} = \frac{3}{2}$ (i.e., there is not a linear speedup with two processors working in parallel). What happens to each policy's ranking with regard to throughput, response time, and wait time?

2.4 *** Do the rankings of throughput hold for all values of λ? Justify your answer fully.

2.5 *** What happens to the throughput rankings as a) μ_t changes; b) μ_b changes; and c) μ_e changes?

2.6 **** If a register fails at rate f and the repair time takes $\frac{1}{r}$ time units, which of the five systems is "best"? Show all of your work.

2.7 ** Consider the shortest-line system (system SL) in which the little rails that keep customers from jumping lines are removed. Suppose that customers in one line, upon seeing that the other line is shorter, switch lines. Does throughput improve or degrade, and by how much?

2.8 ** Consider a new scheme, *longest-line*, where arriving customers go to the longest line. Analyze this scheme and compare it to the other five schemes.

chapter three

Processor
Scheduling

PROBLEM

Vanderbilt's Funniest Dorm Videos, a new local television show, is starting production soon. Viewers send in dorm video recordings, which if they're funny or interesting enough will be included in one of the shows. The producers of the show have been soliciting for video tapes for several months now, and there are shelves and shelves of dorm videos to be screened.

Since the show is locally produced and hasn't even aired yet, the budget is somewhat restricted. The producers were able to afford only one VCR, which is shared between two people, Sarah and Fred, who screen the videos. Each screener retrieves the next tape to be screened from the shelves and goes to the VCR to view it. If both screeners are ready to view a tape, they have to share the VCR. (Whenever only one screener is ready to view a tape, there is no problem.) Fred has more experience and is a faster screener than Sarah. There are many ways for Sarah and Fred to share (i.e., or schedule) the VCR between them.

The analogy to operating systems is clear. Several jobs may be in the ready queue at the CPU. The jobs have different known run times. The job priorities may be different. The issue is to compare various scheduling policies quantitatively.

The scheduling policies being considered by the producers are:

- *First-come-first-served (FCFS).* If Sarah is using the VCR and Fred walks up, then Fred has to wait for Sarah to finish before he can use it (and vice versa).
- *Longest-job-first (LJF).* The slowest person, Sarah, always has priority use of the VCR. If Fred is using the VCR and Sarah walks up, then Fred must remove his tape and let Sarah use the VCR until she is finished. After she leaves, Fred can continue viewing his tape. If Sarah is using the VCR and Fred walks up, Fred must wait until Sarah is finished.
- *Shortest-job-first (SJF).* This is analogous to longest-job-first, except that the faster person (Fred) has priority.
- *Last-come-first-served (LCFS).* The newly arriving screener always has priority. If the VCR is free upon arrival, the screener begins. If the VCR is not free upon arrival, the screener currently using the VCR is preempted and must wait until the arriving screener has finished.
- *Round-robin (RR).* Use of the VCR is doled out in equally sized "chunks" of time, known as *time quanta*. The total time needed to view a tape can be expressed in the (possibly fractional) number of quanta it will take. Once a time quantum is started, it cannot be interrupted until (1) time runs out, or (2) the tape is finished. If there is another person waiting to use the VCR at the end of a quantum, the current VCR user must switch places with the waiting person and a new quantum is begun.

The following parameter values and assumptions are made:

- The average time it takes to get a tape from the shelf is 15 minutes.
- It takes Sarah an average of 1 hour to view a tape.
- It takes Fred an average of 40 minutes to view a tape.
- The time it takes to insert or eject a tape from the machine is negligible.

These measurement parameters characterize the workload and are available by including suitable monitors within the system.

Which scheduling policy results in the most tapes processed? Which scheduling policy is the most fair? Which scheduling policy is the best choice with respect to the number of tapes processed and fairness?

3.1 APPLICATION TO OPERATING SYSTEMS

Multiprogramming allows several jobs to utilize various resources in a computer system simultaneously. This improves the utilization of each resource (i.e., one job can be using the CPU while another is using the disk—both resources are utilized). When designing a multiprogrammed system, difficult problems arise when more than one job competes for the same resource. Some mechanism must exist for sharing the device among competing jobs. For example, when there is more than one job at the CPU, there must be an algorithm that decides which job receives service next. In this chapter we compare different CPU scheduling algorithms and their effects on the performance of the system.

3.2 SOLVING THE ALTERNATIVE MODELS

As usual, let's first decide on symbols to represent the different quantities in the problem. If the unit of time is 1 hour, these quantities have been measured and are known:

- $D_s = 1/\mu_s = 1$: service time of the slower screener (Sarah)
- $D_f = 1/\mu_f = \frac{2}{3}$: service time of the faster screener (Fred)
- $\lambda = 4$: rate at which new tapes are retrieved

In the sno-cone problem of Chapter 1 we compared performance of a system when a slow worker (i.e., server) was employed versus when a fast worker (i.e., server) was employed. Customers of the sno-cone stand were all the same in that they bought identical sno-cones. In this problem there is only one server, the VCR, but the customers are different. (Sarah and Fred place different service demands on the VCR.) Here the goal is to compare system performance when the scheduling policy governing use of the shared device (VCR) is changed. When all the customers are treated exactly the same, as in the sno-cone problem, the system is referred to as a *single-class system*. That is, there is a single class of customers and they all "look" alike to the worker (meaning that it will take the same average amount of time to service that customer as it would any customer).

Single-class systems are said to satisfy the *homogeneous workload* assumption—all jobs look alike in that they place statistically identical demands on the resources.

In this problem, however, there are two classes of customers: slow (Sarah) and fast (Fred), with one customer in each class. Whenever customers do not receive the same average service at a device, the system is referred to as being *multiclass*. Multiclass systems are more complicated than single-class systems in that each class of customers will have its own throughput and response time. This leads to issues of fairness when working with multiclass systems. Systems that give preference to one class of customers over another (thereby increasing the chosen class's throughput) are less fair than systems that schedule resources without regard to a customer's class.

The objective is to determine which scheduling policy will result in the most tapes processed, which policy is the most fair, and which policy gives the best compromise between throughput and fairness. The average number of tapes processed per hour is the throughput of the system. Solving for system throughputs was considered in previous sections and seems solvable. But how should "fairness" be defined quantitatively? One could say that a system is fair when every customer, regardless of class, spends the same amount of time waiting for and using the VCR. (That is, the system is fair if the average response time for every customer is identical.) Fast customers might complain about this interpretation. They would argue that they are being penalized because they are fast. ("Why should I have to wait longer because somebody else is less efficient than I am?") Alternatively, one could say that a system is fair when the ratio of the amount of time a person spends at the VCR (response time) to the amount of time actually spent using the VCR (service time) is the same for all people. Deciding which scheme is best overall (i.e., gives best throughput and is the most fair) is an issue we will defer for now. First, we must solve for throughputs and response times of each system. Not only will there be a global, systemwide throughput and response time, but each class of customer will also have its own throughput and response time.

Actually, in single-class systems, the queueing discipline doesn't matter. Since all customers are statistically identical, shuffling customers within the queue has no effect upon the *average* behavior. That is, first-come-first-served, last-come-first-served, round robin, and so on, will all give the same performance. The queueing discipline is important only in multiclass systems.

3.2.1 First-Come-First-Served

FCFS is the scheduling policy that has been implicitly assumed. It is a very natural policy and is used often in everyday life. Under this policy, a person arriving at the VCR must wait in line, moving up in line until it is his or her turn to receive service. With FCFS, once a person begins to use the VCR, he or she may not be interrupted. In this example there will never be more than one person waiting to use the VCR. The important features of FCFS are that priority use of the VCR is given to the earliest arrival, and that use of the VCR is nonpreemptive.

Figure 3.1 shows the state transition diagram for the video system when the VCR is scheduled FCFS. Each state is labeled with two letters. The first letter indicates what the slow person (Sarah) is doing when the system is in that state, and the second letter indicates what the fast person (Fred) is doing. The letter "G" indicates the person is getting a new tape from the shelves. The letter "V" indicates that the person is actively using the VCR to view a tape. The letter "W" indicates that the person has a tape but is waiting for his or her turn to use the VCR.

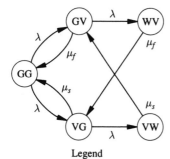

Legend
The first letter indicates the status of the slower
job (Sarah) and the second letter indicates the status
of the faster job (Fred). G = getting a new tape,
V = viewing a tape, W = waiting to view a tape.

Figure 3.1   State Transition
Diagram for FCFS

The steady-state equations for solving this diagram are

$$\mu_s P_{VW} = \lambda P_{VG}$$

$$(\lambda + \mu_s) P_{VG} = \mu_f P_{WV} + \lambda P_{GG}$$

$$2\lambda P_{GG} = \mu_s P_{VG} + \mu_f P_{GV}$$

$$(\lambda + \mu_f) P_{GV} = \mu_s P_{VW} + \lambda P_{GG}$$

$$\mu_f P_{WV} = \lambda P_{GV}$$

$$\sum P_{xy} = 1$$

The solution set for this system is

P_{VW}

$$= \frac{\lambda^2 \mu_f (2\lambda + \mu_f)}{2\lambda^3 \mu_s + 2\lambda^3 \mu_f + \lambda^2 \mu_s^2 + 4\lambda^2 \mu_s \mu_f + \lambda^2 \mu_f^2 + 2\lambda \mu_s^2 \mu_f + 2\lambda \mu_s \mu_f^2 + \mu_s^2 \mu_f^2}$$

P_{VG}

$$= \frac{\lambda \mu_s \mu_f (2\lambda + \mu_f)}{2\lambda^3 \mu_s + 2\lambda^3 \mu_f + \lambda^2 \mu_s^2 + 4\lambda^2 \mu_s \mu_f + \lambda^2 \mu_f^2 + 2\lambda \mu_s^2 \mu_f + 2\lambda \mu_s \mu_f^2 + \mu_s^2 \mu_f^2}$$

P_{GG}

$$= \frac{\mu_s \mu_f}{2\lambda^2 + \lambda \mu_s + \lambda \mu_f + \mu_s \mu_f}$$

P_{GV}

$$= \frac{\lambda \mu_s \mu_f (2\lambda + \mu_s)}{2\lambda^3 \mu_s + 2\lambda^3 \mu_f + \lambda^2 \mu_s^2 + 4\lambda^2 \mu_s \mu_f + \lambda^2 \mu_f^2 + 2\lambda \mu_s^2 \mu_f + 2\lambda \mu_s \mu_f^2 + \mu_s^2 \mu_f^2}$$

P_{WV}

$$= \frac{\lambda^2 \mu_s (2\lambda + \mu_s)}{2\lambda^3 \mu_s + 2\lambda^3 \mu_f + \lambda^2 \mu_s^2 + 4\lambda^2 \mu_s \mu_f + \lambda^2 \mu_f^2 + 2\lambda \mu_s^2 \mu_f + 2\lambda \mu_s \mu_f^2 + \mu_s^2 \mu_f^2}$$

Using $\mu_s = 1$, $\mu_f = \frac{3}{2}$ and $\lambda = 4$ yields

$$P_{VW} = \frac{304}{667}$$

$$P_{VG} = \frac{76}{667}$$

$$P_{GG} = \frac{1}{29}$$

$$P_{GV} = \frac{72}{667}$$

$$P_{WV} = \frac{192}{667}$$

Thus:

- 45.6% of the time Sarah is viewing a tape while Fred is waiting to use the VCR.
- 11.4% of the time Sarah is viewing a tape and Fred is retrieving a tape.
- 3.4% of the time both Sarah and Fred are retrieving tapes.
- 10.8% of the time Fred is viewing a tape while Sarah is retrieving a tape.
- 28.8% of the time Fred is viewing a tape while Sarah is waiting to use the VCR.

The utilization law also applies to finding throughputs of a particular class of customers in a multiclass system. The formula $U = XD$ (i.e., utilization is the product of throughput and demand) becomes $U_i = X_i D_i$, where the subscript i indicates the class of interest. For example, to find Sarah's throughput, the equation is rewritten as

$$X_s = \frac{U_s}{D_s}$$

Therefore, to find Sarah's throughput, we first find Sarah's utilization, then substitute that into the utilization law. (Sarah's demand, D_s, is a known input parameter obtained by measurement.) Fred's throughput is calculated in a similar manner. Sarah's utilization of the VCR can be determined by summing the probabilities of states in which Sarah is actively viewing a tape—that is, any state with a V as the first letter of the state label (i.e., P_{VW} and P_{VG}). These calculations are given in Table 3.1.

TABLE 3.1   Utilization and Throughput Calculations for FCFS

Attendant	Utilization	Throughput
Sarah	$U_s = P_{VW} + P_{VG}$ $= \dfrac{304}{667} + \dfrac{76}{667}$ $= \dfrac{380}{667}$	$X_s = \dfrac{U_s}{D_s}$ $= \dfrac{380/667}{1}$ $= 0.5697$
Fred	$U_f = P_{WV} + P_{GV}$ $= \dfrac{192}{667} + \dfrac{72}{667}$ $= \dfrac{264}{667}$	$X_f = \dfrac{U_f}{D_f}$ $= \dfrac{264/667}{\frac{2}{3}}$ $= 0.5937$

3.2.2 Longest-Job-First

In the LJF scheduling policy, whenever there is more than one person at the VCR, the person that will take the longest (i.e., Sarah) has priority, regardless of the order of arrival. If Fred is using the VCR and Sarah arrives, Fred must immediately stop and relinquish control. Fred will be allowed to finish later when he is the only (i.e., slowest) person at the VCR. This characteristic of the scheduling policy, where one person may be preempted and later restarted, is known as *preemptive resume* (i.e., longest-job-first-preemptive-resume).

Actually, for each of the policies LJF, SJF and LCFS there is a preemptive and a nonpreemptive version. When a scheduling policy is preemptive, processing is interrupted immediately upon arrival of a new customer and service is given to the customer with highest priority. When a scheduling policy is nonpreemptive, the processor is rescheduled only after the current customer finishes service. Since there are only two customers in this system, studying the nonpreemptive versions of these policies will yield the same results as FCFS.

We are also taking liberty by using the term *resume*. A true preemptive resume policy is one in which a preempted process "picks up where it left off" when it gets the processor again. Our model is really a preemptive *restart* model, since a preempted process draws a new service time from the exponential distribution when it is given the processor again. However, preemptive resume and preemptive restart are equivalent in the case of the exponential distribution, due to its memoryless property.

Figure 3.2 shows the state transition diagram for LJF. The state labels are the same as with FCFS. The steady-state equations for solving this diagram are

$$(\lambda + \mu_s)P_{VG} = \lambda P_{GG}$$

$$2\lambda P_{GG} = \mu_s P_{VG} + \mu_f P_{GV}$$

$$(\lambda + \mu_f)P_{GV} = \lambda P_{GG} + \mu_s P_{VW}$$

$$\mu_s P_{VW} = \lambda P_{VG} + \lambda P_{GV}$$

$$\sum P_{xy} = 1$$

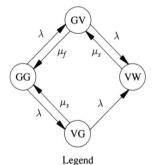

Legend
The first letter indicates the status of the slower job (Sarah) and the second letter indicates the status of the faster job (Fred). G = getting a new tape, V = viewing a tape, W = waiting to view a tape.

Figure 3.2 State Transition Diagram for LJF

The solution set for this system is

$$P_{VG} = \frac{\lambda \mu_s \mu_f}{2\lambda^3 + 3\lambda^2 \mu_s + \lambda^2 \mu_f + \lambda \mu_s^2 + 2\lambda \mu_s \mu_f + \mu_s^2 \mu_f}$$

$$P_{GG} = \frac{\mu_s \mu_f}{2\lambda^2 + \lambda \mu_s + \lambda \mu_f + \mu_s \mu_f}$$

$$P_{GV} = \frac{\lambda \mu_s (2\lambda + \mu_s)}{2\lambda^3 + 3\lambda^2 \mu_s + \lambda^2 \mu_f + \lambda \mu_s^2 + 2\lambda \mu_s \mu_f + \mu_s^2 \mu_f}$$

$$P_{VW} = \frac{\lambda^2 (2\lambda + \mu_s + \mu_f)}{2\lambda^3 + 3\lambda^2 \mu_s + \lambda^2 \mu_f + \lambda \mu_s^2 + 2\lambda \mu_s \mu_f + \mu_s^2 \mu_f}$$

Substituting $\mu_s = 1$, $\mu_f = \frac{3}{2}$ and $\lambda = 4$ yields

$$P_{VG} = \frac{4}{145}$$

$$P_{GG} = \frac{1}{29}$$

$$P_{GV} = \frac{24}{145}$$

$$P_{VW} = \frac{112}{145}$$

The calculations of utilizations and throughputs are given in Table 3.2.

TABLE 3.2   Utilization and Throughput Calculations for LJF

Attendant	Utilization	Throughput
Sarah	$U_s = P_{VW} + P_{VG}$	$X_s = \dfrac{U_s}{D_s}$
	$= \dfrac{112}{145} + \dfrac{4}{145}$	$= \dfrac{116/145}{1}$
	$= \dfrac{116}{145}$	$= 0.8000$
Fred	$U_f = P_{GV}$	$X_f = \dfrac{U_f}{D_f}$
	$= \dfrac{24}{145}$	$= \dfrac{24/145}{\frac{2}{3}}$
		$= 0.2482$

3.2.3 Shortest-Job-First

SJF is analogous to LJF except that priority is given to Fred (i.e., the shortest/fastest job) when both Fred and Sarah want to use the VCR. Figure 3.3 shows the state transition diagram for SJF. It is the same diagram as for LJF, except that the roles of the two customers have been reversed.

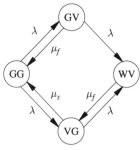

Legend
The first letter indicates the status of the slower
job (Sarah) and the second letter indicates the status
of the faster job (Fred). G = getting a new tape,   **Figure 3.3**   State Transition
V = viewing a tape, W = waiting to view a tape.   Diagram for SJF

The steady-state equations for solving this diagram are

$$(\lambda + \mu_f)P_{GV} = \lambda P_{GG}$$

$$2\lambda P_{GG} = \mu_f P_{GV} + \mu_s P_{VG}$$

$$(\lambda + \mu_s)P_{VG} = \lambda P_{GG} + \mu_f P_{WV}$$

$$\mu_f P_{WV} = \lambda P_{GV} + \lambda P_{VG}$$

$$\sum P_{xy} = 1$$

The steady-state solution is

$$P_{GV} = \frac{\lambda \mu_s \mu_f}{2\lambda^3 + \lambda^2 \mu_s + 3\lambda^2 \mu_f + 2\lambda \mu_s \mu_f + \lambda \mu_f^2 + \mu_s \mu_f^2}$$

$$P_{GG} = \frac{\mu_s \mu_f}{\lambda \mu_s + \mu_s \mu_f + 2\lambda^2 + \lambda \mu_f}$$

$$P_{VG} = \frac{\lambda \mu_f (2\lambda + \mu_f)}{2\lambda^3 + \lambda^2 \mu_s + 3\lambda^2 \mu_f + 2\lambda \mu_s \mu_f + \lambda \mu_f^2 + \mu_s \mu_f^2}$$

$$P_{WV} = \frac{\lambda^2 (2\lambda + \mu_s + \mu_f)}{2\lambda^3 + \lambda^2 \mu_s + 3\lambda^2 \mu_f + 2\lambda \mu_s \mu_f + \lambda \mu_f^2 + \mu_s \mu_f^2}$$

Substituting $\mu_s = 1$, $\mu_f = \frac{3}{2}$, and $\lambda = 4$ yields

$$P_{GV} = \frac{8}{319}$$

$$P_{GG} = \frac{1}{29}$$

$$P_{VG} = \frac{76}{319}$$

$$P_{WV} = \frac{224}{319}$$

The calculations of utilizations and throughputs are given in Table 3.3.

TABLE 3.3 Utilization and Throughput Calculations for SJF

Attendant	Utilization	Throughput
Sarah	$U_s = P_{VG}$	$X_s = \dfrac{U_s}{D_s}$
	$= \dfrac{76}{319}$	$= \dfrac{76/319}{1}$
		$= 0.2382$
Fred	$U_f = P_{WV} + P_{GV}$	$X_f = \dfrac{U_f}{D_f}$
	$= \dfrac{224}{319} + \dfrac{8}{319}$	$= \dfrac{232/319}{\frac{2}{3}}$
	$= \dfrac{232}{319}$	$= 1.0909$

3.2.4 Last-Come-First-Served

LCFS is a preemptive scheduling policy that gives priority to the last customer to arrive at the VCR. The state transition diagram for LCFS is shown in Figure 3.4 and is analogous to that of FCFS. The steady-state equations are as follows:

$$\mu_f P_{WV} = \lambda P_{VG}$$

$$(\lambda + \mu_s) P_{VG} = \mu_f P_{WV} + \lambda P_{GG}$$

$$2\lambda P_{GG} = \mu_s P_{VG} + \mu_f P_{GV}$$

$$(\lambda + \mu_f) P_{GV} = \lambda P_{GG} + \mu_s P_{VW}$$

$$\mu_s P_{VW} = \lambda P_{GV}$$

$$\sum P_{xy} = 1$$

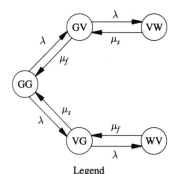

Legend

The first letter indicates the status of the slower
job (Sarah) and the second letter indicates the status
of the faster job (Fred). G = getting a new tape,
V = viewing a tape, W = waiting to view a tape.

Figure 3.4   State Transition
Diagram for LCFS

The steady-state solution is

$$P_{WV} = P_{VW} = \frac{\lambda^2}{2\lambda^2 + \lambda\mu_s + \lambda\mu_f + \mu_s\mu_f}$$

$$P_{VG} = \frac{\lambda\mu_f}{2\lambda^2 + \lambda\mu_s + \lambda\mu_f + \mu_s\mu_f}$$

$$P_{GG} = \frac{\mu_s\mu_f}{2\lambda^2 + \lambda\mu_s + \lambda\mu_f + \mu_s\mu_f}$$

$$P_{GV} = \frac{\lambda\mu_s}{2\lambda^2 + \lambda\mu_s + \lambda\mu_f + \mu_s\mu_f}$$

Substituting $\mu_s = 1$, $\mu_f = \frac{3}{2}$, and $\lambda = 4$ yields

$$P_{WV} = P_{VW} = \frac{32}{87}$$

$$P_{VG} = \frac{4}{29}$$

$$P_{GG} = \frac{1}{29}$$

$$P_{GV} = \frac{8}{87}$$

The calculations of utilizations and throughputs are given in Table 3.4.

3.2.5 Round Robin

In RR, service is doled out in chunks of time called *time quanta*. When a
screener's quantum expires, the VCR is rescheduled. When multiple screeners

TABLE 3.4   Utilization and Throughput Calculations for LCFS

Attendant	Utilization	Throughput
Sarah	$U_s = P_{VW} + P_{VG}$	$X_s = \dfrac{U_s}{D_s}$
	$= \dfrac{32}{87} + \dfrac{4}{29}$	$= \dfrac{44/87}{1}$
	$= \dfrac{44}{87}$	$= 0.5057$
Fred	$U_f = P_{WV} + P_{GV}$	$X_f = \dfrac{U_f}{D_f}$
	$= \dfrac{32}{87} + \dfrac{8}{87}$	$= \dfrac{40/87}{\frac{2}{3}}$
	$= \dfrac{40}{87}$	$= 0.6896$

are waiting to use the VCR, each is allocated a time quantum in a cyclic fashion. That is, the VCR is "time-shared" among the waiting screeners.

The evaluation of RR can be complicated by considering the priority of requests. That is, when a quantum expires, the next quantum is allocated to the waiting customer with the highest priority. Most implementations give the next quantum to the customer that has been waiting the longest for a quantum. This scheme is assumed here. However, any arbitrary priority scheme could be used with a possibly significant effect on overall system performance.

The evaluation of RR is inherently complicated due to the variability of the size of the time quantum. How long should the time quantum be? We consider several values. Two obvious values to consider are zero and infinity, since they are the two extremes and should bound performance. We also consider a value between zero and infinity. This gives three points at which to evaluate RR, which is sufficient to provide general conclusions about the performance of the policy.

First, consider an infinite quantum length. An infinite quantum length will always be longer than the service requirement of any job that arrives at the VCR. This means that a screener using the VCR will never be interrupted by the quantum expiring (i.e., no preemption). When the VCR is rescheduled, it will be given to the screener who has been waiting longest. In other words, RR with an infinite quantum size is identical to FCFS. We have already considered that system in Section 3.2.1.

Next, consider the case where the quantum size is less than infinity but greater than zero. Obviously, we should choose a quantum size that is less than the length of the longest job (to get something different from FCFS). Suppose that the quantum size is 50 minutes. This is a value between the average longest job (i.e., Sarah's 60-minute viewing) and the average shortest job (i.e., Fred's 40-minute viewing). This means that Sarah will take (on average) $\frac{6}{5}$ quanta per visit to the VCR and Fred will take (on average) $\frac{4}{5}$ quanta. Let:

- $Q = \frac{6}{5}$: the rate (i.e., quanta per hour) at which full quanta are completed. (One quantum per 50 minutes is one quantum per $\frac{5}{6}$ hour which implies $\frac{6}{5}$ quanta per hour.)

- $Q_s = 1/(1/\mu_s - 1/Q) = 6$: the rate at which the slow screener (Sarah) finishes her last fractional quantum. (Her last fractional part is $60 - 50 = 10$ minutes. One fractional quantum per 10 minutes implies one fractional quantum per $\frac{1}{6}$ hour, which implies six fractional quanta per hour.)

- $Q_f = \mu_f = \frac{3}{2}$: the rate at which the fast screener (Fred) finishes his last (i.e., only) fractional quantum.

Figure 3.5 is the state transition diagram for this system. The subscripts to the letters "V" and "W" indicate which quantum of service is being waited upon or received. For example, $V_2 W_1$ indicates that Sarah is active at the VCR in the second (i.e., fractional) quantum of service and Fred is waiting to begin the first quantum of service. Sarah will always use one full quantum followed by a fractional quantum of size $1/Q_s$ hours. Fred never uses a full quantum, only a partial quantum of size $1/Q_f$ hours.

We are taking several mathematical liberties here. For instance, the size of a time quantum, $1/Q$, is usually considered to be a constant value. The analysis we are doing here assumes that the quantum size is exponentially distributed with mean $1/Q$. Also, we (at least implicitly) assumed that the time required to view a tape is exponentially distributed. For the slower person, we are now assuming that the time required is the sum of two exponentials (i.e., a full quantum followed by a fractional quantum). Even though the average viewing time is unchanged, the distribution is changed. (It is now assumed to be hypo-exponentially distributed.) Thus we are bending the truth somewhat to keep the analysis tractable. However, the results will still give us a good general idea of how RR behaves. The usefulness (and insight) given by this type of "back-of-the-envelope" mathematics should not be underestimated.

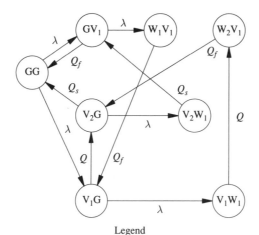

Legend

The first letter indicates the status of the slower job (Sarah)
and the second letter indicates the status of the faster job (Fred).
G = getting a new tape, V_i = viewing a tape in the ith quantum
of service, W_i = waiting for ith quantum of service to begin.

Figure 3.5   State Transition Diagram for RR

The steady-state equations for round robin are:

$$Q_f P_{W_1 V_1} = \lambda P_{GV_1}$$

$$(\lambda + Q) P_{V_1 G} = Q_f P_{W_1 V_1} + \lambda P_{GG}$$

$$Q P_{V_1 W_1} = \lambda P_{V_1 G}$$

$$(\lambda + Q_f) P_{GV_1} = Q_s P_{V_2 W_1} + \lambda P_{GG}$$

$$2\lambda P_{GG} = Q_s P_{V_2 G} + Q_f P_{GV_1}$$

$$Q_s P_{V_2 W_1} = \lambda P_{V_2 G}$$

$$(\lambda + Q_s) P_{V_2 G} = Q P_{V_1 G} + Q_f P_{W_2 V_1}$$

$$Q_f P_{W_2 V_1} = Q P_{V_1 W_1}$$

$$\sum P_{xy} = 1$$

The resulting symbolic values of the solution are rather long and complicated
and are omitted here. However, solving these equations and substituting $Q = \frac{6}{5}$,
$Q_s = 6$, $Q_f = \frac{3}{2}$, and $\lambda = 4$, the steady-state probabilities are

$$P_{W_1 V_1} = \frac{5824}{31,949}$$

$$P_{V_1 G} = \frac{2850}{31,949}$$

$$P_{V_1 W_1} = \frac{9500}{31,949}$$

$$P_{G V_1} = \frac{2184}{31,949}$$

$$P_{GG} = \frac{1521}{31,949}$$

$$P_{V_2 W_1} = \frac{988}{31,949}$$

$$P_{V_2 G} = \frac{1482}{31,949}$$

$$P_{W_2 V_1} = \frac{7600}{31,949}$$

The calculations of utilizations and throughputs are given in Table 3.5.

TABLE 3.5 Utilization and Throughput Calculations for RR

Attendant	Utilization	Throughput
Sarah	$U_s = P_{V_1 G} + P_{V_1 W_1}$ $+ P_{V_2 W_1} + P_{V_2 G}$ $= \frac{2850}{31,949} + \frac{9500}{31,949}$ $+ \frac{988}{31,949} + \frac{1482}{31,949}$ $= \frac{14,820}{31,949}$	$X_s = \frac{U_s}{D_s}$ $= \frac{14,820/31,949}{1}$ $= 0.4638$
Fred	$U_f = P_{W_1 V_1} + P_{G V_1}$ $+ P_{W_2 V_1}$ $= \frac{5824}{31,949} + \frac{2184}{31,949}$ $+ \frac{7600}{31,949}$ $= \frac{15,608}{31,949}$	$X_f = \frac{U_f}{D_f}$ $= \frac{15,608/31,949}{2/3}$ $= 0.7327$

Finally, consider the case where the quantum size approaches zero. Recall the infinite quantum size case: With an infinite quantum size, RR degenerates to FCFS. Now consider this system during a period of time in which no new customers arrive and no customers depart (i.e., the number of screeners at the VCR remains constant). If we look at the amount of service time each screener gets during this time, we will see that with an infinite quantum size one screener (the first one in line) is getting everything. As the quantum size gets smaller and the screeners need more than one quantum to finish, the amount of service given to each screener becomes more uniform. In the limit as the quantum size approaches zero, the amount of service given to each screener, provided that there are no arrivals or departures, is exactly the same.

> To determine the rate at which a customer finishes at a processor-shared server, one simply divides the rate at which the customer would finish if it had the entire server to itself by the number of customers currently at the server (including itself).

Suppose that there are two people at the VCR and the quantum size approaches zero. If nobody arrives or leaves within the next 30 minutes, both will receive 15 minutes of service in that time. As another way to think about this, if there are two people at the VCR, each will proceed at a rate that is half as fast as if they had the VCR to themselves.

> In PS environments, the power of the server is divided equally among the customers at the server. Each customer's service rate is divided by the number of customers present at any point in time.

When the quantum size approaches zero, RR degenerates to a scheme known as processor sharing (PS). Processor sharing is a mathematical abstraction—you cannot really have a quantum size of zero.

> The reason a zero quantum size is unrealistic is that in any system, no matter how efficient, there will be overhead involved in context switching (i.e., where one screener relinquishes control of the VCR, unloads the tape, and lets another person load their tape and begin viewing). If this overhead is anything other than zero, response time for all customers is infinite. The choice of quantum size for an implementation of RR ultimately depends on the overhead involved in context switching and how fair the system should be to its customers. Smaller quantum sizes result in fairer systems, but performance decreases as more time is spent in context switching.

However, the solution to PS is much easier to obtain than for RR with nonzero quantum sizes. (We did not even write out the symbolic solution since it was quite complex.) Therefore, PS is often used to obtain approximate solutions for RR systems. Figure 3.6 shows the state transition diagram for PS. Note that when both screeners are using the VCR (state VV), their respective rates of flow out of that state are reduced by half (i.e., their respective service times are doubled).

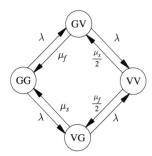

Legend

The first letter indicates the status of the slower
job (Sarah) and the second letter indicates the status
of the faster job (Fred). G = getting a new tape,
V = viewing a tape, W = waiting to view a tape.

Figure 3.6 State Transition Diagram for PS

The steady-state equations for solving the PS diagram are

$$2\lambda P_{GG} = \mu_s P_{VG} + \mu_f P_{GV}$$

$$(\lambda + \mu_s) P_{VG} = \lambda P_{GG} + \frac{\mu_f}{2} P_{VV}$$

$$(\lambda + \mu_f) P_{GV} = \lambda P_{GG} + \frac{\mu_s}{2} P_{VV}$$

$$\frac{\mu_s + \mu_f}{2} P_{VV} = \lambda P_{GV} + \lambda P_{VG}$$

$$\sum P_{xy} = 1$$

The solution set is

$$P_{GG} = \frac{\mu_s \mu_f}{2\lambda^2 + \lambda \mu_s + \lambda \mu_f + \mu_s \mu_f}$$

$$P_{VG} = \frac{\lambda \mu_f}{2\lambda^2 + \lambda \mu_s + \lambda \mu_f + \mu_s \mu_f}$$

$$P_{GV} = \frac{\lambda \mu_s}{2\lambda^2 + \lambda \mu_s + \lambda \mu_f + \mu_s \mu_f}$$

$$P_{VV} = \frac{2\lambda^2}{2\lambda^2 + \lambda \mu_s + \lambda \mu_f + \mu_s \mu_f}$$

Substituting $\mu_s = 1$, $\mu_f = \frac{3}{2}$, and $\lambda = 4$ yields

$$P_{GG} = \frac{1}{29}$$

$$P_{VG} = \frac{4}{29}$$

$$P_{GV} = \frac{8}{87}$$

$$P_{VV} = \frac{64}{87}$$

The calculations of throughputs and utilizations are given in Table 3.6. Notice that the utilization of the VCR is divided between the two screeners when they are both using the VCR (i.e., each screener utilizes the VCR half of the time when the system is in state VV). Also notice that the solution to PS is identical to the solution found for LCFS.

That LCFS and PS are identical is not by coincidence. Without going into un-needed (unwanted?) detail, there is a set of systems with certain assumptions, known as *product form systems*, in which PS and LCFS always yield identical performance. This raises an interesting aspect, however. Even though PS is unre-alizable because of context switching overhead, LCFS has the same performance and is realizable. So why don't more systems use LCFS? (This is not a rhetorical question. There are good reasons why LCFS is not used in practice.)

TABLE 3.6   Utilization and Throughput Calculations for PS

Attendant	Utilization	Throughput
Sarah	$U_s = \dfrac{P_{VV}}{2} + P_{VG}$	$X_s = \dfrac{U_s}{D_s}$
	$= \dfrac{64/87}{2} + \dfrac{4}{29}$	$= \dfrac{44/87}{1}$
	$= \dfrac{44}{87}$	$= 0.5057$
Fred	$U_f = \dfrac{P_{VV}}{2} + P_{GV}$	$X_f = \dfrac{U_f}{D_f}$
	$= \dfrac{64/87}{2} + \dfrac{8}{87}$	$= \dfrac{40/87}{\frac{2}{3}}$
	$= \dfrac{40}{87}$	$= 0.6896$

3.3 COMPARING THE SYSTEMS

The values required to do comparisons include throughputs at the VCR for each customer (i.e., Sarah's throughput and Fred's throughput), overall throughput at the VCR (i.e., throughput of both Sarah and Fred), and response times for each customer. Total throughput is the sum of throughputs over all customer classes. Therefore, to find the total throughput of a system, we add together Sarah's throughput and Fred's throughput, both of which have already been computed.

Response time for a customer is obtained by applying Little's result using the throughput and average line lengths for that customer. Little's result equates a customer's response time to the average number of customers at the VCR divided by the customer's throughput. The average number of people (i.e., the line length) at the VCR for each customer type is obtained by summing the products of each state's probability and the number of people of that type at the VCR. For example, under the FCFS policy, the average number of slow customers using the VCR at any time (i.e., the percentage of time Sarah is at the VCR) is

$$0P_{GG} + 1P_{VG} + 0P_{GV} + 1P_{VW} + 1P_{WV} = 0.8575$$

Therefore, by Little's result, under FCFS, Sarah's response time is $0.8575/0.5697 = 1.5052$ hours. Table 3.7 shows the total throughput, line length, and response time for each system.

A quick glance at this table shows that LCFS and PS have the same performance measures, although their state transition diagrams (compare Figures 3.4 and 3.6) are dissimilar. In the rest of our discussion, we'll refer to them together as LCFS/PS unless it is necessary to make a distinction.

3.3.1 Ranking by Throughput

In terms of the total number of tapes processed per time unit, the ranking of scheduling policies from best to worst is SJF, RR, LCFS/PS, FCFS, and LJF. Intuitively this makes sense. Suppose that there are two systems, one with only the fast screener and another with only the slow screener. The fast screener's system will have a higher throughput because it takes less time for a tape to be processed. In the SJF system, the fast screener experiences the same performance as if he or she were the only screener in the system. What little time the slow screener is allowed, when the system would otherwise be idle, increases total throughput even more. A similar argument explains why LJF exhibits the worst performance. The other policies fall between these two extremes. In terms of total throughput, a good scheduling scheme (SJF) gives roughly a 30% improvement over a poor scheme (LJF).

TABLE 3.7 Performance Comparisons for the Video Problem

Policy	Throughput			Line Length			Response Time		
	Slow	Fast	Total	Slow	Fast	Total	Slow	Fast	Total
FCFS	0.5697	0.5937	1.1634	0.8575	0.8516	1.7091	1.5052	1.4343	1.4691
LJF	0.8000	0.2482	1.0482	0.8000	0.9379	1.7379	1.0000	3.7789	1.6580
SJF	0.2382	1.0909	1.3291	0.9404	0.7273	1.6677	3.9148	0.6667	1.2548
LCFS	0.5057	0.6896	1.1954	0.8736	0.8276	1.7012	1.7274	1.2001	1.4231
RR	0.4638	0.7327	1.1966	0.8840	0.8168	1.7008	1.9056	1.1148	1.4214
PS	0.5057	0.6896	1.1954	0.8736	0.8276	1.7012	1.7274	1.2001	1.4231

3.3.2 Ranking by Fairness

Even though SJF gives significantly higher throughput, it is strongly biased against screeners who use the VCR for a long time (i.e., Sarah). In other words, SJF is unfair. Two ways to measure fairness seem natural. The first is to define a fair system as being one in which all customers have the same response time. The second is to define a fair system as being one in which the ratio of a customer's response time to that customer's service time is the same for all customers.

The objective function "fairness" has several natural interpretations. The two interpretations presented here are common ones.

Table 3.8 shows two calculations: (1) the differences in response times between Sarah and Fred (F_1), and (2) the differences in the ratios of response time to service time for Sarah and Fred (F_2). The closer these fairness measures are to zero, the fairer the scheduling policy. According to the first method, F_1, FCFS is the most fair, followed by LCFS/PS, RR, LJF, and SJF. The second method, F_2, ranks the policies LCFS/PS, RR, FCFS, SJF, and LJF.

TABLE 3.8   Fairness Measures

Policy	F_1	F_2
FCFS	0.0709	0.6463
LJF	2.7789	4.6684
SJF	3.2481	2.9148
LCFS/PS	0.5273	0.0728
RR	0.7913	0.2339

3.3.3 The Best Compromise

The producers of *Vanderbilt's Funniest Dorm Videos* have asked us to determine which scheduling policy is the best compromise between throughput and fairness. When ranking systems by throughput, a higher throughput value is considered better. When ranking systems by fairness, a lower fairness value is considered better. What is needed is an objective function that rewards better (i.e., higher) throughput and better (i.e., lower) fairness. The function

$$g_i(X, F_i) = \frac{X + K_1}{F_i + K_2}$$

achieves this goal. K_1 and K_2 are nonnegative constants that weight X (i.e., throughput) and F_i (i.e., fairness) appropriately. For example, if K_1 is large (i.e., when K_1 dominates X but K_2 does not dominate F_i), the objective function is biased toward fairness, since a small change in fairness significantly affects the objective function. Similarly, if K_1 is small and K_2 is large, the objective function is biased toward throughput since it is more sensitive to X. By adjusting K_1 and K_2, an objective function can be constructed that is appropriate for any particular application. Table 3.9 shows the comparative results of the policies for g_1 and g_2 with $K_1 = 0$ and $K_2 = 1$.

TABLE 3.9   Values of g_i when $K_1 = 0$ and $K_2 = 1$

Policy	g_1	g_2
FCFS	1.0863	0.7067
LJF	0.2774	0.1849
SJF	0.3129	0.3395
LCFS/PS	0.7827	1.1143
RR	0.6680	0.9698

3.4 RECOMMENDATIONS TO THE PRODUCERS

In our report to the producers, we would recommend that SJF be used to schedule the VCR if simply the total number of tapes to be processed is to be maximized. However, we will point out that if SJF is used, Sarah will be treated unfairly. We would describe the various definitions of fairness, and then recommend FCFS, LCFS, and RR as being policies that are more fair than SJF but at roughly a 10% performance (i.e., throughput) penalty. We would not recommend PS. Although the problem statement says that the amount of time it takes to switch users of the VCR is negligible, in reality there is overhead involved in context switching. In the case of RR with a very small quantum size (i.e., PS), any overhead will result in large response times for all customers. LCFS (which has the same performance as PS) has lower overhead than PS. LCFS requires a context switch whenever a customer arrives or departs. As the load increases, LCFS incurs more overhead.

> A study of actual implementations of operating systems will reveal that these two policies (FCFS and RR), and combinations and variations thereof, are indeed the most widely used scheduling policies, especially for interactive systems.

EXERCISES

3.1 ** Explain why LCFS and PS have the same performance. Will they *always* have the same performance?

3.2 ** LCFS is a realizable policy (i.e., it can be implemented in real computer systems) but PS is a mathematical abstraction that cannot really be implemented. Both policies give the same performance. Why is LCFS rarely used to schedule processes in operating systems? (*Hint*: Consider cases in which service demands of customers are very different.)

3.3 *** Do the relative rankings of the scheduling policies change if the amount of time it takes to get a tape $(1/\lambda)$ changes?

3.4 *** Evaluate the function g using different values of K_1 and K_2. Discuss how the ratio K_1/K_2 affects the the value of the function. Are there any "threshold" values for this ratio where the emphasis on throughput and fairness shifts more dramatically than for other values? Assess the robustness of the thresholds (i.e., evaluate the thresholds for various values λ, μ_s, and μ_f).

3.5 ** g, the function for determining the system that is the best compromise was developed *ad hoc*. Can you propose a better function?

3.6 * Explain how overhead affects the choice of quantum size in round-robin scheduling.

3.7 * Suppose that there are many customers in a system, each with a different service demand at the VCR. If RR is implemented with some quantum size q, which customers will be given preferential treatment?

3.8 ** An aggregate performance measure is a function of the performance measure for all customer classes. In this problem we examined total throughput, total line length, and total response time, all of which are aggregate performance measures. Some analysts believe that aggregate performance measures are useful, whereas others say they are misleading. Give arguments supporting both points of view.

3.9 *** The multilevel feedback queue is an extension to the round-robin scheduling discipline. Consider a system of two queues (lines), where the first queue is managed FIFO and the second queue is managed RR. When a quantum is scheduled, priority is given to the first queue. Only when the first queue is empty will the quantum be given to the customer at the head of the second queue. Newly arrived customers join the first queue. Those customers requiring more than one quantum of service join the second queue after receiving their first quantum and remain in the second queue until service is completed. Such a system is an example of a multilevel feedback queue. (Sometimes this is also referred to as a foreground/background queue.) Determine the state transition diagram for this system and solve for all performance and fairness measures. Compare this system with the other scheduling disciplines. Under what conditions and objective functions would a multilevel feedback queue be desirable? Discuss the impact of the following parameters on the behavior of a multilevel feedback system: number of queues, quantum size, quantum count threshold at which customers join another queue, bi- or unidirectional movement between queues (i.e., the ability to join only a lower-priority queue versus the ability to join either a higher- or a lower-priority queue).

3.10 ** Consider a new scheme, *Random*, where whenever screeners arrive at the VCR they will begin using the VCR if it is free. If a screener arrives at the VCR when the VCR is being used by the other screener, a coin will be flipped regarding who has priority. That is, with probability 0.5, the arriving screener will preempt, and with probability 0.5 the arriving screener will have to wait until the VCR becomes free. Do the analysis for this scheme and compare it to the other six schemes.

chapter four

Disk Scheduling

PROBLEM

Joe is a traveling radio transmitter repairperson responsible for a transmitter in Memphis, a transmitter in Nashville and a transmitter in Knoxville. The three cities are located on Interstate 40, with Memphis to the west of Nashville, and Knoxville to the east of Nashville. The distance between Memphis and Nashville is roughly equal to the distance between Nashville and Knoxville.

> The operating system counterpart to this problem is a computer system having a CPU and a three-cylinder disk drive. There are three processes (customers) in the system. Process 1 has files on cylinder 1. Process 2 has files on cylinder 2. Process 3 has files on cylinder 3. The CPU generates requests for disk service (i.e., the cities generate requests for repairs). The transmitter repairperson in the problem represents the read-write head, which moves from cylinder to cylinder servicing I/O requests.

Joe's job is to drive along Interstate 40 between the three cities servicing transmitters when they break down. When there are no transmitters to be repaired, Joe can be found soaking up the sunshine beside the hotel pool in the last city he visited. When there is only one transmitter on the blink, Joe's next destination is obvious. However, when one or more transmitters is in need of service, the next city to be visited is not clear. One ordering of the cities may result in getting all the repairs completed in the shortest amount of time. However, that ordering could cause some cities to wait a long time to have their transmitter repaired, even though they may have been the first to request a service visit.

This, again, refers to the trade-off between total system throughput and fairness.

Whenever Joe is on his way from Memphis to Knoxville (or vice versa) he passes through Nashville and will always stop in Nashville for a coffee break before continuing his journey.

Joe has four ways (policies) in which he could determine the next city to visit:

- *First-come-first-served (FCFS)*. Joe repairs transmitters strictly in the order in which they break down.

- *Shortest-seek-time-first (SSTF)*. The next transmitter Joe repairs is always the closest one. This includes a distance of 0 (the closest broken transmitter is the one in the current city). If Joe is in Nashville and both Knoxville's and Memphis's transmitters are down (but Nashville's is not), he flips a coin to decide which to repair first (since both are the same distance away).

- *SCAN*. At any given time, Joe has a "preferred traveling direction," which is either east or west. If there is a transmitter to be repaired in a city in the preferred direction, Joe travels toward that city. (If a broken transmitter is in the current city, it is considered to be in the preferred direction.) If there are broken transmitters, but none of them is in the preferred direction, the preferred direction is reversed.

- *Circular SCAN (C-SCAN)*. The preferred direction is always east. (If a broken transmitter is in the current city, it is considered to be in the preferred direction.) When there are no service requests to the east, Joe chooses to repair next the transmitter in the westernmost city requesting service. If Joe is in Knoxville and there is a request in Memphis, he will travel to Memphis via Nashville but will not spend time repairing Nashville's transmitter on the way.

Actually, the schemes described here are LOOK and C-LOOK, variations of SCAN and C-SCAN. In pure SCAN, the drive head sweeps the entire surface of the disk, visiting the outermost (respectively, innermost) cylinder before changing direction, even if there is no pending request at the outermost (respectively, innermost) cylinder. In pure C-SCAN the drive head sweeps from the innermost cylinder to the outermost cylinder (as in pure SCAN) and returns to the innermost cylinder to start the next scan, regardless of whether there is a pending request at that cylinder. Making use of the information about which cylinders have pending requests to determine "how far to go" in a direction transforms SCAN and C-SCAN to LOOK and C-LOOK. When SCAN and C-SCAN are referred to, one normally assumes LOOK and C-LOOK, as in this problem.

The following information is given:

- The transmitters in Memphis and Nashville have a mean time to failure of $\frac{7}{10}$ of a day from the time of the last repair to the next failure. The Knoxville transmitter is a newer, more reliable model with a mean time to failure of $\frac{7}{3}$ days.
- The mean travel time between adjacent cities is 1 day. (Travel between Memphis and Knoxville is via Nashville and takes 2 days.)

In any disk system with a moving read/write head, the seek time between cylinders takes a significant amount of time. This "traveling" time should be minimized.

- The mean time to repair a transmitter is 1 hour.

Which policy results in the most total "uptime" for all transmitters? Which policy is the most fair? [A totally fair system would ensure that the mean time between when a service visit is requested and the time when the repair is completed (i.e., response time) is the same for all cities.] Which policy provides the best trade-off between total uptime and fairness?

In this problem, a definition of fairness is given (unlike the VCR problem, where a definition was left unspecified). It should be noted, however, that other definitions of fairness could be applied (i.e., one might weight response times by the failure rate, meaning that transmitters that break down less often should be allowed to enjoy decreased response times).

4.1 APPLICATION TO OPERATING SYSTEMS

Just as processes contend for use of the CPU (see Chapter 3), they also contend for usage of auxiliary storage devices, such as a disk drive. In this problem we analyze the various disk scheduling strategies. The three cities correspond to three regions (e.g., cylinders or tracks) of a disk. Joe, the repairperson, represents the read/write head, which moves between the cylinders servicing requests. A transmitter failure corresponds to a read/write request for the corresponding disk cylinder.

For the CPU scheduling problem of Chapter 3, the cost of context switching (i.e., the time required to stop service to one process and begin the service of another) is relatively small with respect to the service time. In processor scheduling, this is typically the case where the operating system overhead for a context switch is small. In I/O scheduling, however, the cost of context switching is relatively high with respect to the service time, since the time to move the head between cylinders is much greater than the time it takes to read or write to a cylinder. This increased overhead cost, due to the inherent characteristics of disk storage devices, makes many of the CPU scheduling algorithms (e.g., any preemptive algorithm) unfeasible for disk scheduling. Other scheduling algorithms must be considered.

4.2 COMPARISON WITH THE VCR SCHEDULING PROBLEM

This problem is a scheduling problem similar to the VCR problem of Chapter 3. Several alternative scheduling policies are offered and the issues of throughput and fairness must be addressed. As discussed in the VCR problem, fairness is only an issue in systems where there exists a distinction between the various customers (i.e., a multiclass system).

Each of the three processes is in a separate customer class. Each process is allowed to have its own disk access frequency and each process is allowed to have its own disk access properties. In this example, process 1 (Memphis) has a mean disk interaccess time of $\frac{7}{10}$ and always accesses cylinder 1. Process 2 (Nashville) has a mean disk interaccess time of $\frac{7}{10}$ and always accesses cylinder 2. Process 3 (Knoxville) has a mean disk interaccess time of $\frac{7}{3}$ and always accesses cylinder 3.

This traveling repairperson problem is multiclass for two reasons: (1) not all transmitters have the same mean time to failure, and (2) each transmitter is in a different city whose geographic location will affect the frequency with which Joe is in town. Joe may have a tendency to discriminate against the outlying cities (Memphis and Knoxville) and favor the middle city (Nashville) simply because, in order to travel from Memphis to Knoxville, or vice versa, he will pass through Nashville. Certain of the policies allow Joe to repair a transmitter in the current city, regardless of the time it failed. This will encourage discrimination against certain cities. Because of their different locations, certain cities will experience different repair response times.

In the VCR problem it was possible for the two screeners to "time-share" the VCR because the time to perform a context switch was negligible.

The VCR problem is concerned with processor scheduling, where the context switch time is small. This problem is concerned with disk scheduling, where the overhead time to switch between requests may be large.

In this problem, a context switch is analogous to traveling from one city to another. The overhead incurred is significant. Therefore, policies that involve preemption and time sharing (e.g., round robin and preemptive-resume policies) are not feasible. That is, it is rather foolish to start repairing the transmitter in Nashville, stop in the middle, go to Memphis to start repairing the transmitter there, stop in the middle, come back to Nashville to continue, stop, return to Memphis, and so on, when the average time to repair a transmitter is 1 hour and the average time to travel between cities is 1 day. All of the policies presented here implicitly assume that once a repair (i.e., service) is begun, it cannot be interrupted.

In the VCR problem, the VCR did not change state. It remained the same regardless of who used it last. In this problem, however, Joe can be in one of three different cities at any given time, depending on the last transmitter that was serviced. Thus the time required to service the next request depends not only on the type of request (i.e., where Joe must go) but also on the current state (i.e., where Joe is currently). Such state-dependent behavior is common.

The position of the read/write head (i.e., the state of the disk) affects the response time of the next request.

4.3 SOLVING THE ALTERNATIVE MODELS

For each scheduling policy alternative, an appropriate state diagram can be constructed. From each state diagram the values necessary to compute uptime (i.e., the amount of time in which a transmitter is functioning) and response time (i.e., the time between failure of a transmitter and the completion of its repair) for each policy can be obtained. Throughout the analysis, the following symbols and associated values will be used. All rates are with respect to weekly periods.

1. $\lambda_1 = \lambda_2 = 10$: rate at which transmitters in Memphis and Nashville fail
2. $\lambda_3 = 3$: rate at which the transmitter in Knoxville fails
3. $\mu_t = 7$: rate at which travel between adjacent cities is completed
4. $\mu_r = 168$: rate at which a transmitter is repaired

Some critics may be disturbed by modeling travel between cities as proposed here. Suppose that Joe begins to travel from Memphis to Nashville, but before he arrives in Nashville, some other event occurs (i.e., another transmitter breaks down). In all of our models it will be as if Joe had never left Memphis!

Again, the memoryless property of the exponential distribution is the reason for this model of travel behavior. We have mentioned the "memoryless property" before. It roughly means that when a change in state occurs, all the "timers" are restarted (i.e., all information about the preceding state of the system is forgotten — only the current state is important).

This is stretching the truth. (We have been doing that with all of our models, we are just stretching a little further here.) However, overly harsh criticism is unwarranted. First, the problem could have been posed differently, where instead of driving between cities, Joe could have gone to the local airport and waited for the next flight. If an event happened (e.g., another transmitter failed) while at the airport, Joe could change his plans immediately. Second, the state diagrams (to follow) could have been changed to include "in-transit" states to model travel more accurately.

> There are yet other (minor) model inaccuracies. Actual disk drives do not cause the read/write head to stop at intermediate cylinders when seeking between nonadjacent cylinders. The models here, although consistent throughout all alternatives, are not absolutely accurate in all respects. The trade-off between complexity and accuracy is a common one in performance evaluation and system modeling.

This would allow more accurate models at the price of added complexity. The added complexity is not worth it. (Take our word for it!) Third, as long as *consistency* is maintained between the various models, their *relative* performance will remain consistent. It is this relative comparison that is important here, not absolute accuracy of each model.

4.3.1 First-Come-First-Served

Figure 4.1 shows the algorithm that implements FCFS as would be executed by Joe. If there are no pending requests, then Joe remains in the last city he visited, waiting for a service call. When a service call comes in, Joe travels to that city (if it is not the current city). He may have to pass through other cities to get to his destination. Once he arrives at his destination he immediately starts effecting repairs. During any of this time other transmitters may break down. The order in which they fail is noted. Joe may only re-

```
Initially
    Joe is in Memphis
    No transmitters are broken
Loop
    If no transmitter is broken
        Then lounge by the pool
    Else
        Travel to the city whose transmitter has been broken the longest
            and repair it
Endloop
```

Figure 4.1   First-Come-First-Served

pair transmitters in the order of failure. This means that if he passes through a city with a broken transmitter while on the way to repair another, earlier request, he is not allowed to repair the newer request even though he is in town.

Figure 4.2 is a partial state transition diagram for FCFS. Each state is labeled with four numbers, three on top and one below. The top three numbers indicate which cities have reported a failure and are waiting for a repair visit. The numbers 1, 2, and 3 are associated with the cities Memphis, Nashville, and Knoxville, respectively. The number 0 is not associated with any city and functions as a placeholder. The single bottom number indicates Joe's current location. Furthermore, the order in which the numbers appear indicates the order in which the failures occurred, with the rightmost number being associated with the oldest pending request. If a city's number appears on the bottom row, Joe is in that city when the system is in that state. For example, the state $\binom{032}{1}$ indicates that Nashville and Knoxville are both requesting a visit, with Nashville's request being the oldest and Joe's current location being Memphis.

The diagram is partial because not all states and transitions are shown. The complete diagram consists of 48 states and 90 arcs. Of those 48, the 16 states in which Joe is in Nashville are shown in the diagram.

Since the diagram is large, so also is the set of balance equations needed to solve it. Therefore, the equations are not given here. Needless to say, solving the system of 48 equations manually is quite tedious. However, several linear algebra packages exist that can easily solve these equations. The steady-state probability for each state is given in Table 4.1.

Part of learning the "art" of performance evaluation is learning the tools of the trade. Systems of interest will probably be too large to solve by hand. Even the simple systems we are dealing with may require the aid of a "solver" package. The purpose of this book is not to teach methods for solving systems of linear equations; rather, it is to show how solving these systems can be used as a tool for obtaining performance measures of computer systems.

Ultimately, we wish to rank the different policies by total uptime (i.e., the sum of the mean uptimes for each transmitter) and fairness (i.e., the variance of the mean response times for each transmitter repair). To find the uptime for each city, the sum of the probabilities of being in states in which that city is not awaiting or receiving repair service should be summed. This sum gives the fraction of a week in which the transmitter in that city is working properly. Recalling that the numbers 1, 2, and 3 correspond to the cities Memphis, Nashville

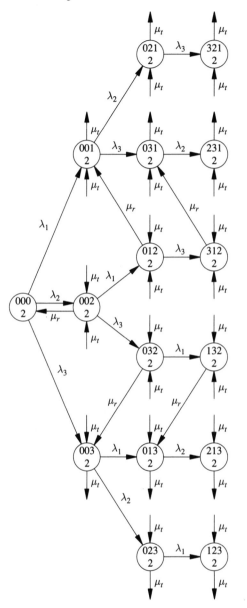

Legend

The top three digits indicate pending requests in the order received (from right to left). Zero functions as a place holder. The bottom digit indicates Joe's current location.

Figure 4.2   Partial Diagram for FCFS

and Knoxville, respectively, the uptime for Memphis is given by the expression:

$$\sum_{i=1}^{3} \left(\begin{array}{c} P[S000 - i] + P[S002 - i] + P[S003 - i] \\ + P[S023 - i] + P[S032 - i] \end{array} \right) = 0.2168$$

TABLE 4.1 Steady-State Probabilities for FCFS

State	Prob.	State	Prob.	State	Prob.	State	Prob.
S000-1	0.0248	S012-1	0.0448	S031-1	0.0012	S213-1	0.0084
S000-2	0.0253	S012-2	0.0042	S031-2	0.0281	S213-2	0.0547
S000-3	0.0044	S012-3	0.0524	S031-3	0.0023	S213-3	0.0024
S001-1	0.0034	S013-1	0.0059	S032-1	0.0337	S231-1	0.0019
S001-2	0.0524	S013-2	0.0324	S032-2	0.0014	S231-2	0.0435
S001-3	0.0132	S013-3	0.0013	S032-3	0.0015	S231-3	0.0033
S002-1	0.0448	S021-1	0.0039	S123-1	0.0349	S312-1	0.0192
S002-2	0.0035	S021-2	0.0894	S123-2	0.0614	S312-2	0.0018
S002-3	0.0086	S021-3	0.0529	S123-3	0.0026	S312-3	0.0224
S003-1	0.0100	S023-1	0.0245	S132-1	0.0481	S321-1	0.0026
S003-2	0.0144	S023-2	0.0185	S132-2	0.0022	S321-2	0.0610
S003-3	0.0006	S023-3	0.0008	S132-3	0.0022	S321-3	0.0227

That is, the transmitter in Memphis is up for 21.68% of the time on the average. Another way to think of this quantity is as a utilization. The transmitter in Memphis is utilized (i.e., is up and being used) with a probability of $U_1 = 0.2168$. Similarly, the uptimes for Nashville and Knoxville transmitters can be found to be $U_2 = 0.2198$ and $U_3 = 0.4280$, respectively. The total uptime, found by summing the individual uptimes, is 0.8646.

> Another interpretation of total uptime is the probability of all three transmitters working properly at the same time. This quantity is equal to $P[S000 - 1] + P[S000 - 2] + P[S000 - 3]$. Using this interpretation would lead to similar comparisons and conclusions.
>
> Although the individual uptimes are indeed utilizations of each transmitter, the total uptime cannot be thought of as a utilization. The concept of utilization usually applies to a single device and is the percentage of time (i.e., probability that) the device is in a state in which it does useful work.

To determine fairness (i.e., the variance of the mean response times for each transmitter repair), we must first find the repair response times for each city. Response times are most easily calculated by using Little's result: Response time equals the ratio of throughput to the average number of outstanding requests. However, this requires that we find the "throughput" of each city. Throughput is the average number of repairs completed each week. Each transmitter will experience a different throughput. The sum of these will be the total throughput, or the average total number of repairs made each week. The utilization law (utilization equals the product of throughput and the mean service demand) is used to determine throughput, as usual. However, there are two ways in which the utilization law can be applied to this problem: (1) using the utilizations of the three transmitters and the demand associated with the failure rate λ_i, and (2) using the utilization of Joe with respect to each transmitter and the demand associated with the rate of repair μ_r. The first way calculates the rate at which transmitters actually fail (not the rate at which they fail when they are functioning properly, which is λ). The second method calculates the rate at which transmitters are actually repaired (not the rate at which they are repaired when they are broken down, which is μ_r). In steady-state, these quantities must be equal, since for every breakdown there will be a repair. We will use the first method since we have already calculated utilizations (i.e., uptime) of each transmitter.

Think of each transmitter as a customer that has its own dedicated server. While the transmitter is receiving service from the dedicated server, it is "up" and functioning properly. The transmitter completes its service (i.e., it fails) at rate λ_i. Therefore, the demand each transmitter places on its dedicated server is $D_i = 1/\lambda_i$. When a transmitter completes its service at the dedicated server, it goes to a repairserver, which is shared by all transmitters (i.e., the repairperson, Joe). Since the repair server is shared among the transmitters, a transmitter may have to wait in line for service. This description of the system, although different from that presented in the problem definition, leads to the same state transition diagram and balance equations. It is, in fact, the same system; it is just described differently. U_1, U_2, and U_3 are the utilizations of the three dedicated servers, which correspond to the uptimes of each transmitter. Viewing the system from this different perspective, we now see that the appropriate demands to use in the utilization law are D_1, D_2, and D_3, where $D_i = 1/\lambda_i$. Therefore, using the first method, throughputs of the FCFS system are

$$X_i = \frac{U_i}{D_i}$$

$$= U_i \lambda_i$$

$$X_1 = 0.2168 \times 10$$

$$= 2.1680$$

$$X_2 = 0.2198 \times 10$$

$$= 2.1980$$

$$X_3 = 0.4280 \times 3$$

$$= 1.2840$$

$$X_{\text{all}} = 2.1680 + 2.1980 + 1.2840$$

$$= 5.6500$$

Therefore, the average number of failures each week is 2.1680 for Memphis, 2.1980 for Nashville, and 1.2840 for Knoxville. The total number of failures is 5.6500 per week. Since flow-in equals flow-out, this means that there are also 5.6500 repairs performed each week.

To use the second method in finding throughputs, we would define utilization as the percentage of time Joe is actively repairing a transmitter, and multiply this by his repair rate.

Response time for each city (i.e., the average amount of time between when a transmitter breaks down and its repair is completed) can be calculated using Little's result. Recall that Little's result states that $N = XR$, where N is the average number of customers in a system, X is the throughput of the system, and R is the response time of the system. In the current application, X is the average number of repairs (or failures) per week (i.e., throughput), R is the time from a failure until its repair (i.e., response time), and N is the average number of outstanding repair requests at any time. When computing the response time for a particular city, N is a number between 0 and 1, since at any time, at most one repair is outstanding for that city. Therefore, N is simply the probability that the transmitter of interest is broken. Thus N is the downtime percentage and is equal to 1 minus the uptime percentage (i.e., $1 - U$, which is the idle time of the transmitter).

$$R_i = \frac{N_i}{X_i} = \frac{1 - U_i}{X_i}$$

$$R_1 = \frac{1 - 0.2168}{2.1680} = 0.3612$$

$$R_2 = \frac{1 - 0.2198}{2.1980} = 0.3549$$

$$R_3 = \frac{1 - 0.4280}{1.2840} = 0.4454$$

Similarly, the overall response time equals the ratio of the average number of outstanding repairs in all cities to the average number of total repairs per week.

Overall response time is not the straight average of the individual response times, since some cities have more repairs than others. The individual response times should be weighted by the city throughputs. This leads to an alternative calculation of overall response time, which is

$$R_{\text{all}} = \sum_{i=1}^{3} \left(\frac{X_i}{X_{\text{all}}} \right) R_i$$

The average number of outstanding repairs equals the average number of transmitters which are down, which equals three minus the average number of transmitters which are up (i.e., $3 - 0.8646 = 2.1354$). The average number of total repairs per week is $X_{\text{all}} = 5.6500$. Thus

$$R_{\text{all}} = \frac{2.1354}{X_{\text{all}}} = 0.3779$$

The more alike the response times of the three cities are, the more fair the policy is. We use the following function of response times (standard deviation for a set of measurements) to quantify fairness. The smaller the value of the function, the more alike the response times are and the fairer the policy is.

$$F = \sqrt{\frac{1}{3} \sum_{i=1}^{3} \left(R_i - \frac{\sum_{j=1}^{3} R_j}{3} \right)^2}$$

For FCFS,

$$F = \sqrt{\frac{1}{3} \left(\begin{array}{c} (0.3612 - 0.3871)^2 + (0.3549 - 0.3871)^2 \\ + (0.4454 - 0.3871)^2 \end{array} \right)}$$

$$= \sqrt{0.0017}$$

$$= 0.0412$$

Table 4.2 summarizes the results of the calculations for FCFS.

4.3.2 Shortest-Seek-Time-First

The SSTF policy is implemented by the algorithm given in Figure 4.3. If the transmitter in the current city is broken, it is considered to be the closest and is repaired first. In the event that there are two broken transmitters at the same

TABLE 4.2   Summary of Measures for FCFS

Measure	Memphis	Nashville	Knoxville	Overall
U (utilization)	0.2168	0.2198	0.4280	0.8646
X (throughput)	2.1680	2.1980	1.2840	5.6500
R (resp., time)	0.3612	0.3549	0.4454	0.3779
F (fairness)				0.0412

```
Initially
    Joe is in Memphis
    No transmitters are broken
Loop
    If no transmitter is broken
        Then lounge by the pool
    Else
        Travel to the nearest city whose transmitter
        is broken and repair it
Endloop
```

Figure 4.3   Shortest-Seek-Time First

distance from Joe's current position, Joe flips a coin to decide which city to visit next. (This situation occurs when Joe is in Nashville and there are broken transmitters in Memphis and Knoxville but not in Nashville.)

A partial diagram for SSTF is given in Figure 4.4. The meaning of the state descriptions is the same as in the FCFS diagram of Figure 4.2 except that, since the order of failure is unimportant, the top row of numbers is always ordered in ascending sequence. The eight states in which Joe is in Nashville are shown in the diagram. The complete diagram has 24 states and 58 arcs. Note that the two arcs departing state $\binom{013}{2}$ are labeled with rate $\mu_t/2$. These two arcs go to states $\binom{013}{1}$ and $\binom{013}{3}$ (not shown in the diagram). These arcs represent the case when Joe has to toss a coin to decide which way to travel next. There is a probability of $\frac{1}{2}$ that he will go to Memphis and a probability of $\frac{1}{2}$ that he will go to Knoxville. In this case, μ_t is "spread out" equally over two arcs. The steady-state probabilities for all states are given in Table 4.3.

TABLE 4.3   Steady-State Probabilities for SSTF

State	Prob.	State	Prob.	State	Prob.	State	Prob.
S000-1	0.0694	S002-1	0.0774	S012-1	0.0051	S023-1	0.1116
S000-2	0.0433	S002-2	0.0059	S012-2	0.0129	S023-2	0.0084
S000-3	0.0213	S002-3	0.0140	S012-3	0.0962	S023-3	0.0004
S001-1	0.0095	S003-1	0.0471	S013-1	0.0063	S123-1	0.0071
S001-2	0.1466	S003-2	0.0691	S013-2	0.1791	S123-2	0.0114
S001-3	0.0484	S003-3	0.0029	S013-3	0.0045	S123-3	0.0020

Uptime (utilization), throughput, and response time are calculated as with the FCFS system. Table 4.4 shows the results of these calculations.

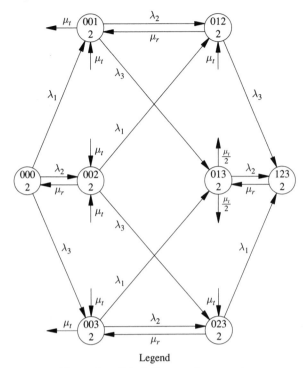

Legend

The top three digits indicate pending requests.
Zero functions as a place holder. The bottom
digit indicates Joe's current location.

Figure 4.4   Partial Diagram for SSTF

TABLE 4.4   Summary of Measures for SSTF

Measure	Memphis	Nashville	Knoxville	Overall
U (utilization)	0.4708	0.6475	0.5500	1.6685
X (throughput)	4.7089	6.4758	1.6503	12.8350
R (resp., time)	0.1124	0.0544	0.2726	0.1037
F (fairness)				0.0923

4.3.3 SCAN

The algorithm for SCAN is given in Figure 4.5. Under this scheme, Joe has a "preferred direction" in which he will travel as long as there are pending requests in that direction. A city is considered to be in the preferred direction if Joe is in that city. When there are pending requests, but none of them is in the preferred direction, Joe reverses the preferred direction.

A partial diagram for SCAN is given in Figure 4.6. The meaning of the state labels is the same as for SSTF, but there is an arrow to indicate the

Initially
   Joe is in Memphis
   No transmitters are broken
   Preferred direction is east
Loop
   If no transmitter is broken
      Then lounge by the pool
   Else
      Travel to the nearest city in the preferred
         direction whose transmitter is down and repair it.
         (If no request exists in the preferred direction,
         then reverse direction.)
Endloop

Figure 4.5 SCAN

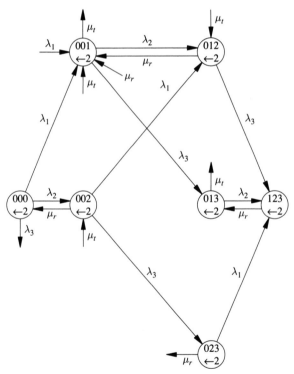

Legend

The top three digits indicate pending requests. Zero functions as a placeholder. ← indicates the preferred direction is west. → indicates the preferred direction is east. The bottom digit indicates Joe's current location.

Figure 4.6 Partial Diagram for SCAN

preferred direction. A left-pointing arrow (←) indicates that Joe's preferred direction is west, and a right-pointing arrow (→) indicates that Joe's preferred direction is east. The seven states in which Joe is in Nashville with a western preferred direction are shown in the figure. The partial diagram in which Joe is in Nashville but moving in a easterly direction would be symmetrical to the partial diagram in Figure 4.6. The complete diagram consists of 30 states and 76 arcs. The steady-state probabilities for the SCAN system are given in Table 4.5. The summary statistics for the system are given in Table 4.6.

TABLE 4.5   Steady-State Probabilities for SCAN

State	Prob.	State	Prob.	State	Prob.	State	Prob.
S000←2	0.0061	S002←3	0.0130	S012→1	0.0054	S023→1	0.1036
S000←3	0.0197	S002→1	0.0816	S012→2	0.0003	S023→2	0.0078
S000→1	0.0732	S002→2	0.0053	S013←2	0.0719	S123←2	0.0045
S000→2	0.0386	S003←3	0.0027	S013←3	0.0051	S123←3	0.0021
S001←2	0.1545	S003→1	0.0412	S013→1	0.0053	S123→1	0.0066
S001←3	0.0525	S003→2	0.0640	S013→2	0.1027	S123→2	0.0066
S001→1	0.0100	S012←2	0.0132	S023←2	0.0000		
S002←2	0.0008	S012←3	0.1013	S023←3	0.0004		

TABLE 4.6   Summary of Measures for SCAN

Measure	Memphis	Nashville	Knoxville	Overall
U (utilization)	0.4580	0.6475	0.5755	1.6810
X (throughput)	4.5803	6.4754	1.7265	12.7822
R (resp., time)	0.1183	0.0544	0.2459	0.1032
F (fairness)				0.0796

4.3.4 Circular SCAN

In C-SCAN, Joe's preferred direction is always east. As long as there is a request in that direction, Joe continues to move easterly making repairs. However, when there are no requests farther east, Joe determines the western-most city requesting service and "locks in" on that city as his next destination, ignoring all other service requests. For instance, Joe will lock in on Memphis when he is in Knoxville, provided that there is no request in Knoxville and there is a request in Memphis. In this case, while Joe is traveling to Memphis via Nashville, he will not repair any transmitter in Nashville while enroute.

Figure 4.7 shows the algorithm for C-SCAN. A partial diagram is given in Figure 4.8 and consists of two parts. The leftmost portion focuses on states where Joe is in Nashville and is not in transit from Knoxville to Memphis (i.e., Joe is not "locked in" on Memphis). The rightmost portion focuses on states

> Initially
>   Joe is in Memphis
>   No transmitters are broken
> Loop
>   If no transmitter is broken
>   Then lounge by the pool
>   Else
>   Travel to the nearest city in the easterly
>   direction whose transmitter is down and repair
>   it. (If no request exists farther east, then travel to the
>   westernmost requesting city without repairing any
>   intermediate transmitters along the way.)
> Endloop

Figure 4.7   Circular SCAN

where Joe is in Nashville but enroute to Memphis to start another scan. The symbol $\otimes$ appearing in a state description indicates that Joe is not allowed to repair a broken transmitter in the current city—he is "locked in" on Memphis and his priority is to get to Memphis before performing any repairs. The complete diagram consists of 28 states and 65 arcs. The steady-state probabilities for C-SCAN are given in Table 4.7 and the performance measures for uptime, throughput, response time, and fairness are shown in Table 4.8.

TABLE 4.7   Steady-State Probabilities for C-SCAN

State	Prob.	State	Prob.	State	Prob.	State	Prob.
S000-1	0.0401	S002-1	0.1100	S012-1	0.0107	S023-1	0.1123
S000-2	0.0576	S002-2	0.0079	S012-2	0.0042	S023-2	0.0078
S000-3	0.0175	S002-3	0.0115	S012-3	0.1088	S023-3	0.0003
S001$\otimes$2	0.0204	S003-1	0.0091	S013$\otimes$2	0.0036	S123$\otimes$2	0.0466
S001-1	0.0055	S003-2	0.0570	S013-1	0.0007	S123-1	0.0089
S001-2	0.0642	S003-3	0.0024	S013-2	0.1218	S123-2	0.0078
S001-3	0.0584	S012$\otimes$2	0.0966	S013-3	0.0059	S123-3	0.0023

TABLE 4.8   Summary of Measures for C-SCAN

Measure	Memphis	Nashville	Knoxville	Overall
U (utilization)	0.4335	0.4642	0.6135	1.5112
X (throughput)	4.3350	4.6424	1.8405	10.8179
R (resp., time)	0.1307	0.1154	0.2100	0.1376
F (fairness)				0.0415

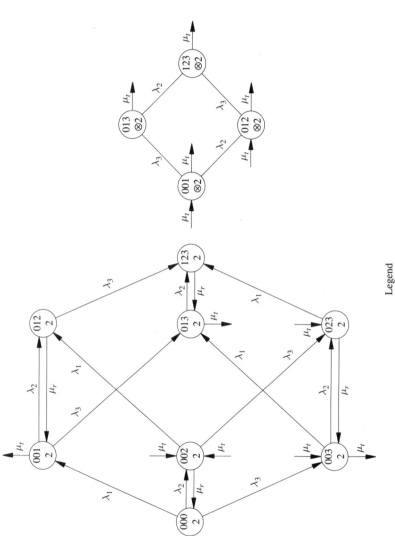

Legend

The top three digits indicate pending requests. Zero functions as a placeholder. ⊗ indicates Joe is "locked in" on a city. The bottom digit indicates Joe's current location.

Figure 4.8　Partial Diagram for C-SCAN

4.4 COMPARING THE ALTERNATIVES

Table 4.9 shows the uptimes, fairness, response times, and throughput measures for each of the four policies. With respect to total uptime, the polices are ranked from best to worst as SCAN, SSTF, C-SCAN, and FCFS. With respect to overall throughput, the same basic ranking holds, with the exception that SSTF is slightly better than SCAN.

The reason that SSTF outperforms SCAN with respect to throughput while SCAN outperforms SSTF with respect to uptime (in this example) is as follows. The only difference in the policies is when the disk head is at cylinder 2 and cylinders 1 and 3 both have outstanding requests. Under SSTF, there is a *slight* bias toward cylinder 1 over cylinder 3 since cylinder 1 makes more frequent requests—increasing overall throughput. SCAN removes this bias, decreasing throughput. However, being biased in favor of cylinder 3 over cylinder 1 improves overall uptime, since cylinder 3 "stays up" longer on average (i.e., cylinder 3 has fewer requests). Thus, servicing cylinder 3 before cylinder 1 improves uptime. SCAN provides this improvement, but at a (slight) reduction in throughput.

TABLE 4.9 Comparison of the Policies

Policy	U_1	U_2	U_3	Total Up-Time	F	R_{all}	X_{all}
FCFS	0.2168	0.2198	0.4280	0.8646	0.0412	0.3779	5.6500
SSTF	0.4708	0.6475	0.5500	1.6685	0.0923	0.1037	12.8350
SCAN	0.4580	0.6475	0.5755	1.6810	0.0796	0.1032	12.7822
C-SCAN	0.4335	0.4642	0.6135	1.5112	0.0415	0.1376	10.8179

This is hardly surprising since uptime and throughput are closely related. (The faster repairs are completed, the more quickly broken transmitters are brought back up.) Under the given conditions, SSTF, SCAN, and C-SCAN all outperform FCFS by a factor of 2.

In general, regardless of the policy imposed, the central region of the disk receives preferential treatment. This is because seek times to the center cylinders are shorter on average. This can be seen by directly comparing cylinders 1 and 2. Each of these has the same service times and the same average times between requests. Cylinder 3 is special since its request rate is much smaller.

Comparing the uptimes of the individual cities we see that even though the Memphis and Nashville transmitters have the same mean time to failure, the uptime for Nashville (U_2) is always better than for Memphis (U_1). This is because the mean distance from any other city to Nashville is less than the mean distance to Memphis. Joe never has to travel more than one step to get to Nashville from any other city. However, in the case of Memphis, Joe may have to travel two steps, which takes longer and reduces the uptime for the outlying Memphis. (This same bias against Knoxville occurs but is counterbalanced due to Knoxville's longer mean time to failure.)

Turning to fairness, FCFS (as expected) gives the best measure of fairness, followed by C-SCAN, SCAN, and SSTF. FCFS and C-SCAN are roughly equivalent with respect to fairness. SCAN and SSTF are significantly less fair than FCFS and C-SCAN. FCFS is fair because the order in which requests are serviced has nothing to do with geographic location. However, FCFS is "stupid" in that Joe is not allowed to repair a transmitter in the current city unless it is first on the list. Since the repair time (1 hour) is much shorter than the travel time between cities (24 hours), it would be more sensible to service the request out of turn. C-SCAN adopts this policy somewhat, but instead of serving requests in the order they are received, C-SCAN serves requests in a static order determined by location. In other words, the three cities are always serviced in the same order: Memphis, Nashville, and Knoxville. In this way, C-SCAN produces better throughput while remaining fair.

In general, the methods of choice are SCAN or C-SCAN, depending on the relative importance of uptime (or, throughput) versus fairness. SCAN provides better uptime and throughput while C-SCAN is fairer. SSTF provides *slightly* better throughput than SCAN, but the drop in fairness is not worth it. Similarly, FCFS is fairer than C-SCAN, but its significant drop in uptime is not worth it.

EXERCISES

4.1 ** Draw the entire state diagrams for each of the scheduling policies: (*a*) FCFS; (*b*) SSTF; (*c*) SCAN; (*d*) C-SCAN.

4.2 ** Redo the analysis of each scheduling policy under the assumption that the transmitter in Memphis does not exist; there are only two cities making requests, Nashville and Knoxville.

4.3 *** Again, consider the Memphis transmitter as being nonexistent. Do a sensitivity analysis of the SSTF policy as the mean time to failure at Knoxville varies from 0 to 3 days (in increments of 0.5 day). Interpret the results.

4.4 **** Write programs to generate listings of the states and arcs for each of the state transition diagrams in the problem. Set up the system of balance equations and use an appropriate solver package to verify the steady-state probabilities given in each of the tables.

4.5 *** It seems that the transmitters are down almost all the time. It takes longer to travel between cities than it does for a transmitter to break down. As the company that manufactures the transmitters improves the quality of its product, does the choice of which scheduling policy is used become more or less important? Substantiate your claim by plotting relative performance versus the mean time to failure for SSTF and C-SCAN.

4.6 ** Under what circumstances (if any) would the "pure" forms of SCAN and C-SCAN be used? By "pure" we mean that all cities in the preferred direction are visited, even if they have no pending request. How would performance be affected if the pure forms were used in this problem?

4.7 *** Given the original problem parameter settings ($\mu_r = 168$, $\mu_t = 7$, $\lambda_1 = \lambda_2 = 10$, and $\lambda_3 = 3$) SSTF, SCAN, and C-SCAN each outperformed FCFS by a factor of 2 with respect to total uptime. In other words, SSTF, SCAN, and C-SCAN produced roughly the same improvement over FCFS. Determine parameter settings that cause the difference between FCFS and the other policies to decrease. Based on your findings, can you formulate basic rules of thumb as to which policy should be used under different general loading conditions?

4.8 **** Suppose that all three transmitters have the same mean failure rate. Recompute the rankings. Is there something special about a three-city (i.e., three disk cylinders) case? If so, explain why this is a special case.

4.9 **** In the conclusion it was explained why FCFS and C-SCAN had comparable fairness measures whereas FCFS had such poor throughput. It was hinted that this may not be the case if the ratio μ_t/μ_r were larger. Explore various ratios to see how sensitive the comparison is to this ratio.

4.10 **** For the FCFS policy, let each transmitter have a mean failure rate of $\lambda = 5$ and solve for overall throughput keeping all other parameters as stated in the original problem. Now, increase λ by 1, solve, and repeat. Make the curve with λ on the horizontal axis and throughput on the vertical axis. An interesting and unexpected phenomenon happens as λ approaches 10. Can you explain this phenomenon? Which of the other two parameters (μ_t and μ_r), if changed, will cause the point at which the phenomenon occurs to move the most? (That is, the phenomenon is most sensitive to which parameter: μ_r or μ_t?)

4.11 *** Analyze "smart FCFS," which is identical to the FCFS described in the problem except that Joe is allowed to service other requests along the way. What parameter of the system must be relatively small to make "smart FCFS" a good choice?

4.12 **** Consider dual-head disks, where there are two read/write arms. (This is analogous to having two independent repairpeople, Joe and Flo.) Perform both quantitative and qualitative analysis assuming (a) a FCFS scheduling policy; (b) SSTF scheduling policy. How do these policies compare with respect to overall throughput, response time, and fairness?

chapter five

Process
Synchronization

PROBLEM

Jill and Bill are the sole sales representatives for the *Encyclopedia Vanderbiltia* company. Each works at home, using a telephone to peddle these "beautiful gold-accented leather-bound 26 volume set[s], sure to enhance your child's educational experience." When a representative makes a sale, she or he calls the corporate office to place the order using the company's voice mail system.

> The operating system issue being addressed is process synchronization. In all operating systems, several processes that use a common resource (hardware or software) must be coordinated so that only a limited number of processes (usually, one process) have simultaneous access to a resource. Deadlock, simultaneous access of the resource by too many processes, indefinite postponement, and starvation of processes must be avoided. Several alternatives exist. We seek to compare their relative performance.

There are 10 mailboxes in the system, numbered 0 to 9. After the system answers the phone, the sales representative selects a mailbox by pressing a digit on the phone's keypad. After selecting the mailbox, the sales representative may either press 0 to listen to the last message left in the box, or 1 to leave a message in that box (any previously existing message in the box is recorded over). Only one mailbox may be checked or changed per call and the system will service only one call at a time. Mailbox 0 is reserved for encyclopedia orders. This mailbox is checked regularly by the corporate office staff. If a message is found in mailbox 0, it is transcribed to a paper order form and the message is erased (a blank message is recorded). The other nine mailboxes are not used.

Originally, when a sale was made, the representative repeatedly called, checking mailbox 0 until it was empty. That is, the voice mail system was called, mailbox 0 was selected, and the "0" was pressed to listen to its contents. Once mailbox 0 was found empty, the voice mail system was called again, this time selecting mailbox 0 and pressing "1" to leave an order message. This scheme was acceptable until the day that Jill's order was lost. Evidently, the following sequence of events took place: (1) Jill and Bill had both made sales, (2) Jill called the voice mail system and found mailbox 0 empty, (3) Bill called in and also found mailbox 0 to be empty, (4) Jill called back and deposited her order, and (5) Bill called back and placed his order, overwriting Jill's.

Needless to say, Jill was not pleased and, after venting her wrath, convinced Bill that a better system was needed to prevent lost orders in the future. Together, the two approached the manager, Ms. Azaelia, who said that the problem should be solved by mutual agreement between the sales representatives, and that they could expect no help from the office staff. However, she suggested that maybe Jill and Bill could use mailboxes 1 through 9 for passing messages between themselves.

Develop a system which ensures that no orders will be lost and yet has acceptable performance given that (on average):

1. One sale is made every 15 minutes when the representative is actively selling.

2. It takes 1 minute to check a mailbox or leave a message.

3. The office staff checks mailbox 0 once every 4 minutes.

5.1 APPLICATION TO OPERATING SYSTEMS

As we have seen repeatedly, many of the problems that arise in the design of multiprogrammed computer systems are those dealing with the sharing of some resource. In Chapter 3 we considered processes competing for a CPU. In Chapter 4 we considered processes competing for a disk drive. In each of these situations, access to the resource was controlled by a central agent. For example, when scheduling the CPU, the operating system scheduler chose the next process to be serviced. The scheduler, not the processes, made the decision. Therefore, control was *centralized* in the scheduler.

In this problem, resource sharing under *distributed* control is considered. That is, the processes themselves make the decision. For the resource to be managed correctly, the processes must work together, agreeing on which of them should have access to the resource. Agreement can come about only by communication among the processes. Areas of computer memory can be set aside for message passing. Processes can read a memory location or they can write to a memory location. The memory locations and the read/write operations are represented by the voice mail system. The 10 mailboxes are 10 memory locations. Listening to a message is analogous to a memory read. Recording a message is analogous to a memory write. The fact that the voice mail system allows only one call at a time reflects the fact that memory accesses in most computer systems are atomic (i.e., uninterruptible) and mutually exclusive (i.e., only one such operation is occurring at any given time).

In this problem we explore several different distributed synchronization algorithms. The merits of each algorithm with respect to performance, correctness, and reliability are assessed.

5.2 Algorithm 1: THE ORIGINAL ALGORITHM

Before proceeding, let's reexamine the algorithm that caused Jill's order to be lost. (See Algorithm 1, shown in Figure 5.1.) Each sales representative follows this algorithm. For Jill's order to be lost, it must have been recorded over by Bill. Neither Jill nor Bill would have left an order message unless she or he had first checked to make sure that mailbox 0 was empty. Here is what happened: Jill checked mailbox 0 and found it empty; Bill checked mailbox 0 and found it empty; Jill left her order; Bill left his order before the office had a chance to pick up Jill's.

This problem can also be viewed as a simple producer/consumer problem, where Jill and Bill are the producers and the corporate office is the consumer. However, we approach the problem as a more general shared resource problem. Mutual exclusion by synchronization is a means by which resource sharing can be controlled.

This problem can be solved by an algorithm that guarantees mutual exclusion; that is, when a sales representative leaves an order message, it is impossible for the other representative to place another order (i.e., overwrite an earlier order) until the previous one has been picked up by the office. Guaranteeing mutual exclusion is a problem of synchronization—coordinating the actions of the two representatives so that mutual exclusion holds for the sensitive part of the algorithm (step C).

STEP	INSTRUCTIONS
A:	Sell.
B:	Repeatedly check the order box until it becomes empty.
C:	Leave an order message and go back to selling (go to A).

Figure 5.1 Algorithm 1 — The Original System

The part of an algorithm that can be executed by at most one person at any given time (in this case, step C) is known as the *critical section* of the algorithm.

In general, a critical section is limited to having at most N people inside (i.e., executing) it simultaneously. The parameter N represents the number of resources being controlled. For this problem, $N = 1$, since there is a single resource, mailbox 0, being controlled. Also, in general, M people may be competing to use the critical section. In this problem, $M = 2$, Jill and Bill.

A general algorithm to solve this problem has four parts:

1. Sell.
2. Enter the critical section and "lock the door."
3. *Critical section*: Leave the order message and wait for it to be picked up, ensuring that it will not be overwritten.
4. "Unlock the door" and exit the critical section.

Steps 2 and 4 work together to ensure mutual exclusion of step 3. Together, they guarantee that at most one person is in the critical section at any time. Steps 2 and 4 should also ensure that a representative, upon finding the critical section locked, will eventually be allowed inside.

5.3 Algorithm 2: TURN-PASSING

Jill and Bill decide to use mailbox 1 to hold a special message which they call the "turn message." The message is either "It is Jill's turn," or "It is Bill's turn." To enter the critical section (CS), a sales representative checks the turn message.

If it is not that representative's turn, she or he waits, repeatedly checking the turn message, until it becomes her or his turn. The critical section is then entered. Upon exiting, the representative changes the turn message to indicate that it is the other representative's turn. This is Algorithm 2, shown in Figure 5.2.

STEP	INSTRUCTIONS
A:	Sell.
B:	Check the turn message. Repeat until it is my turn.
C:	(CS) Leave an order message and wait for it to be picked up.
D:	Change the turn message and go back to selling (go to A).

Initial condition: Turn message = "It is Jill's turn"

Figure 5.2   Algorithm 2 — Turn-Passing

The initial condition states that before any representative begins to execute the algorithm, the turn message is arbitrarily set to "It is Jill's turn." Does this algorithm ensure mutual exclusion? In other words, is it possible for both representatives to execute step C simultaneously? If mutual exclusion does hold, is the performance of the system acceptable? (For example, is the number of encyclopedias sold per unit of time acceptable? Is the system fair?) State transition diagrams can be used to answer these questions.

The behavior of Algorithm 2 is shown in Figure 5.3. Each state of the diagram is labeled with two letters and a number. The first letter indicates which step of the algorithm is currently being executed by Jill, the second letter indicates which step Bill is currently executing, and the number indicates whose turn it is (1 for Jill and 2 for Bill). The rate of flow from one state to another depends on the step being executed. Step A, in which a representative is selling, completes at an average rate of $a = 4$ sales per hour. Step B, in which the turn message is checked, completes at an average rate of $b = 60$ calls per hour. In step C, the order message is placed, picked up by the office staff, and the pickup is verified by the sales representative at an average rate of $c = 10$ times per hour.

> The average time spent at step C is the total average time to make a call (1 minute), have the message picked up (4 minutes), and verify that it was picked up (1 minute).

Step D, in which the turn is changed, completes at a rate of $d = 60$ times per hour.

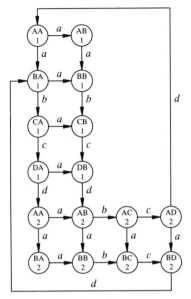

Legend

The first letter indicates which step of Algorithm 2 Jill is executing. The second letter indicates which step of Alorithm 2 Bill is executing. The number indicates the value of the turn message. A "1" indicates "It is Jill's turn." A "2" indicates "It is Bill's turn."

Figure 5.3   Algorithm 2 — State Transition Diagram

The initial state of the system is $\binom{AA}{1}$, where Jill and Bill are each selling and it is (arbitrarily) Jill's turn. From this state, either Jill or Bill will make a sale, each at rate a. If Bill makes the sale and gets to state $\binom{AB}{1}$ he will start checking the turn message. But since it is not his turn, he will not be able to leave step B until Jill has made a sale and passed the turn.

When a representative repeatedly calls to check the turn message only to find that it is not her or his turn, the representative is said to be *spin waiting*. There is no need for arcs in the diagram to show that spin waiting is occurring. These arcs would arrive at the same state from which they departed. For example, there is no arc labeled b from state $\binom{DB}{1}$ because such an arc would lead to state $\binom{DB}{1}$. These looping arcs do not contribute to the solution of the system because they appear on both sides of the balance equation and can be deleted.

Mutual exclusion of the critical section holds for this algorithm because there is no state labeled $\binom{CC}{1}$ or $\binom{CC}{2}$. That is, it is not feasible to enter into any state where more than one person is in the critical section. Solving the balance equations for this system yields a throughput of 3.954 encyclopedia sets sold each hour. This indicates that representatives are spending a large percentage of time waiting to get into the critical section (looping at step B). If there were no waiting, we would expect each representative to cycle through the algorithm in 23 minutes, which would result in 5.217 encyclopedia sets being sold per hour by both Jill and Bill. This is motivation for finding another algorithm with better performance.

> The derivation and solution of the balance equations are left as an exercise. The use of equation-solving packages (e.g., Maple, Mathematica, Eureka!, etc.) are helpful since the solution of these equations can be quite tedious.

5.4 Algorithm 3: VOTING I

The major problem with Algorithm 2 is that if one representative wants to place an order, she or he must wait her or his turn *even if* the other representative does not want to place an order (i.e., the other representative is selling). The voting algorithm, shown in Figure 5.4, corrects this problem. It requires two special mailboxes in addition to mailbox 0. Mailbox 1 will be known as Jill's vote, and mailbox 2 will be known as Bill's vote. A vote of "yes" indicates that a sales representative gives her or his permission for the other representative to enter the critical section. Just prior to entering the critical section, a representative

STEP	INSTRUCTIONS
A:	Sell.
B:	Check other representative's vote. Repeat until it is "yes."
C:	Vote "no."
D:	(CS) Leave an order message and wait for it to be picked up.
E:	Vote "yes" and go back to selling (go to A).

Initial conditions: Jill's vote = Bill's vote = "yes"

Figure 5.4   Algorithm 3 — Voting I

sets her or his vote to "no," denying others permission to enter. Upon exiting the critical section, a representative sets her or his vote to "yes."

Figure 5.5 illustrates the behavior of this algorithm. The diagram at the top, labeled "Bill," is the diagram that Bill is following. The diagram at the left, labeled "Jill," is the diagram that Jill is following. By combining these diagrams, the large diagram labeled "Both Jill and Bill" is produced. (The labels on the arcs in the large diagram have been omitted to make the diagram easier to understand. The labels can be deduced by referring to each representative's diagrams.)

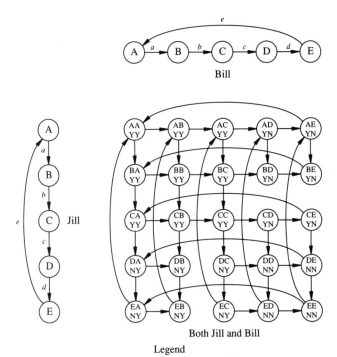

Both Jill and Bill

Legend

The first letter, top row, indicates which step of Algorithm 3 Jill is executing. The second letter, top row, indicates which step of Algorithm 3 Bill is executing. The first letter, bottom row, indicates Jill's vote (Y = yes, N = no). The second letter, bottom row, indicates Bill's vote.

Figure 5.5   Algorithm 3 — State Transition Diagram

The large diagram describes the overall state behavior. Each state is labeled with four letters. The first column is information pertaining to Jill, and the second column is information pertaining to Bill. The top letter is the step that the representative is currently executing, and the bottom letter is the value of that representative's vote. For example, $\binom{DB}{NY}$ represents the state where Jill is executing the critical section, step D, with her permission vote set to "no," while Bill is cycling at step B (waiting for Jill's permission) with his own vote set to "yes." The initial state of the system is $\begin{pmatrix} AA \\ YY \end{pmatrix}$.

An examination of the diagram shows that mutual exclusion does not hold because the state $\begin{pmatrix} DD \\ NN \end{pmatrix}$ can be entered. That is, both representatives could be in the critical section, step D, simultaneously. The sequence of events leading to this state could be: Bill completes step A, Jill completes step A, Bill completes step B, Jill completes step B, Bill completes step C, Jill completes step C, Bill begins step D, and Jill begins step D. This path sequence is

$$\begin{pmatrix} AA \\ YY \end{pmatrix} \rightarrow \begin{pmatrix} AB \\ YY \end{pmatrix} \rightarrow \begin{pmatrix} BB \\ YY \end{pmatrix} \rightarrow \begin{pmatrix} BC \\ YY \end{pmatrix} \rightarrow \begin{pmatrix} CC \\ YY \end{pmatrix} \rightarrow \begin{pmatrix} CD \\ YN \end{pmatrix} \rightarrow \begin{pmatrix} DD \\ NN \end{pmatrix}$$

Since mutual exclusion is not guaranteed, further analysis of this algorithm is of no benefit.

5.5 Algorithm 4: VOTING II

Algorithm 3 suffers from the same problem encountered in Algorithm 1—mutual exclusion is not guaranteed. Algorithm 4, shown in Figure 5.6, is the same as Algorithm 3 except that steps B and C have been interchanged. The behavior of this algorithm is illustrated in Figure 5.7. Since there is no state in the diagram in which both representatives are executing statement D, $\begin{pmatrix} DD \\ ?? \end{pmatrix}$, mutual exclusion is guaranteed.

STEP	INSTRUCTIONS
A:	Sell.
B:	Vote "no."
C:	Check other representative's vote. Repeat until it is "yes."
D:	(CS) Leave an order message and wait for it to be picked up.
E:	Vote "yes" and go back to selling (go to A).

Initial conditions: Jill's vote = Bill's vote = "yes"

Figure 5.6   Algorithm 4 — Voting II

To obtain a measure for throughput, the system of balance equations is formulated and solved for the steady-state probability of being in each state. However, a visual analysis of the diagram gives the same answer with much less effort. Consider state $\begin{pmatrix} CC \\ NN \end{pmatrix}$. Notice that there are two arcs leading into this state but no arc leading out of this state.

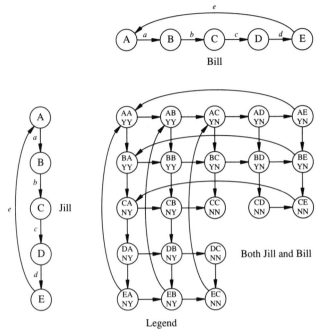

Bill

Jill

Both Jill and Bill

Legend

The first letter, top row, indicates which step of Algorithm 4 Jill is executing. The second letter, top row, indicates which step of Algorithm 4 Bill is executing. The first letter, bottom row, indicates Jill's vote, (Y = yes, N = no). The second letter, bottom row, indicates Bill's vote.

Figure 5.7   Algorithm 4 — State Transition Diagram

> States that have incoming arcs but no outgoing arc are *sink* (i.e., *deadlock*) *states*. Once in such a state, the system remains in that state forever. The steady-state probability of the state is 1. All states that lead to a deadlock state are transient states. Transient states have a steady-state probability of zero.

Since flow into a state must equal the flow out of a state, the flow along both of these input arcs must be zero. As a matter of fact, in steady-state, there is no flow along any arc in the diagram! The probability of being in any state except $\binom{CC}{NN}$ is zero. The probability of being in state $\binom{CC}{NN}$ is 1. That is, once the system gets into state $\binom{CC}{NN}$, the system stays in that state forever.

This condition is better known as *deadlock*, a state in which each representative is waiting on the other to change her or his vote to "yes" with no chance of giving in and letting the other go first. The steady-state probabilities show that at some point in time, this deadlock state will be entered. Once entered, it cannot be exited. No progress is made. Throughput is zero. Therefore, an algorithm with a potential for deadlock is not acceptable.

5.6 Algorithm 5: VOTING III

A third attempt to salvage the voting algorithm produces Algorithm 5, shown in Figure 5.8. The problem with Algorithm 4 was that once a representative voted "no" there was no going back and "giving in" by voting "yes" (until after the critical section was completed). Some courteous way is needed of allowing a representative to say "I want the CS and if you don't want it, I'll use it, but if you want it, please, go ahead of me." Algorithm 5 allows this. In this algorithm, the step executed after step C depends on the value of the other's vote. If the other's vote is "no", step D is next, in which the representative gives in and votes "yes" to let the other representative enter the critical section. If the other's vote is "yes", the critical section can be entered. The behavior of this algorithm is shown in Figure 5.9.

STEP	INSTRUCTIONS
A:	Sell.
B:	Vote "no."
C:	If the other representative's vote is "no," then
D:	Vote "yes" and go to B.
E:	(CS) Leave an order message and wait for it to be picked up.
F:	Vote "yes" and go back to selling (go to A).

Initial conditions: Jill's vote = Bill's vote = "yes"

Figure 5.8   Algorithm 5 — Voting III

A study of the diagram shows that mutual exclusion of the critical section holds because there is no state in which both representatives are executing the critical section, step E. Also, there are no deadlock states. Therefore, the steady-state solution of the balance equations can be derived (the specification and solution of the equations is left as an exercise). The system throughput is 4.406 encyclopedia sets sold each hour. This is a 12% improvement over Algorithm 2. It seems that Algorithm 5 is preferable to Algorithm 2. However, there are problems with Algorithm 5. The rate at which a sale is made is 4 per hour. Suppose that this rate were increased to 60 per hour and Algorithm 2 and Algorithm 5 reevaluated. The analysis would show that Algorithm 5 performs 27% *worse* than Algorithm 2!

The reason is that under the given conditions, representatives spend most of their time selling. (The steady-state probabilities bear this out.)

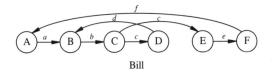

Bill

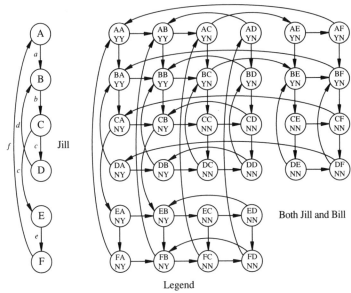

Legend

The first letter, top row, indicates which step of Algorithm 5 Jill is executing. The second letter, top row, indicates which step of Algorithm 5 Bill is executing. The first letter, bottom row, indicates Jill's vote, (Y = yes, N = no). The second letter, bottom row, indicates Bill's vote.

Figure 5.9   Algorithm 5 — State Transition Diagram

> The selling phase is the bottleneck of the system.

The probability that both representatives want in the critical section at the same time is small. In this situation, Algorithm 5 is better than Algorithm 2 since the strict alternation of using the critical section in Algorithm 2 often unnecessarily delays a representative from entering the critical section, hurting performance. However, when the rate at which a sale is made increases, the probability that there will be contention for the critical section increases. In this situation, Algorithm 2 outperforms Algorithm 5, because Algorithm 5 has more overhead for deciding who gets into the critical section. That is, under heavy loading, strict alternation of who is allowed to use the CS is an efficient, effective technique. A look at the diagram of Algorithm 5 shows that there is substantial looping back to previous states. A representative that loops back to step B essentially loses any ground that has been gained and has to start over. This is a case of everyone being too nice ("You go ahead." "No, you go ahead." "No, please! You first!" ...).

> This phenomenon is also referred to as "starvation" or "indefinite postponement." It is usually not a problem, but it is possible, particularly under heavy loads.

Therefore, the algorithm of choice depends on the workload—the rate at which the central office is required (i.e., its utilization).

This excessive looping leads to another problem — progress is not guaranteed in Algorithm 5. It is possible for the two representatives to get into a "lockstep" where each of Jill and Bill votes "no," then checks the other's vote, then both vote "yes," then both loop back ... indefinitely. Lockstep cannot occur in Algorithm 2 since all paths leading back to any previous state will cause at least one encyclopedia set to be sold.

> Our analysis makes the assumption that the step completion times are independent random variables. Because of this independence, being postponed *indefinitely* is not possible. However, being postponed for significant periods of time (while all processes cycle around steps B–C–D) is likely.

5.7 Algorithm 6: DEKKER'S ALGORITHM

Algorithm 6, known as Dekker's algorithm for mutual exclusion, is shown in Figure 5.10. It is a combination of the turn-passing algorithm (Algorithm 2) and the voting algorithms (Algorithms 3 through 5). Algorithm 2 guaranteed mutual exclusion by passing a turn back and forth between the two representatives. Low throughput resulted, however, because sometimes a representative was ready to place an order but was not allowed to, even though the critical section was not in use. The voting algorithms corrected this problem and improved utilization of the critical section. However, problems concerning mutual exclusion, deadlock, or indefinite postponement occurred. Dekker's algorithm takes the best features of the turn-passing and voting algorithms. The turn flag is used only when both

STEP	INSTRUCTIONS
A:	Sell.
B:	Vote "no."
C:	If the other representative's vote is "no," then
D:	If it is my turn, then go to C.
E:	Vote "yes."
F:	Wait for my turn and go to B.
G:	(CS) Leave an order message and wait for it to be picked up.
H:	Pass turn.
I:	Vote "yes" and go back to selling (go to A).

Initial conditions: Jill's vote = Bill's vote = "yes" Turn = Jill's

Figure 5.10   Algorithm 6 — Dekker's Algorithm

representatives need the critical section. In this way, both mutual exclusion and progress are guaranteed.

The state diagram for Dekker's algorithm consists of 122 states and is not shown.

> Instead of drawing a diagram for this algorithm, a short program was written that generated a list of all the states and transitions.

There is no state in which both representatives are executing statement G, the critical section. Therefore, mutual exclusion holds for Dekker's algorithm. Also, there are no deadlock states.

Under the given conditions, Dekker's algorithm has a throughput of 4.192 encyclopedia sets sold per hour, an improvement of 6% over Algorithm 2. However, if the time required to sell each encyclopedia set is decreased to an average of 1 minute per sale (i.e., if the demand of the critical section is increased), the throughput of Algorithm 6 is 5.432. In this situation, the throughputs of Algorithms 2 and 5 would be 7.466 and 5.890, respectively. Therefore, the workload intensity (i.e., the demand for the critical section) directly affects which algorithm is preferable.

5.8 Algorithm 7: PETERSON'S ALGORITHM

Dekker's algorithm (Algorithm 6) has a large state space, which implies that a significant amount of overhead is required to manage the critical section. Peterson has proposed (yet another) algorithm, shown in Figure 5.11. There are seven steps and 58 states, compared to the nine steps and 122 states for Dekker's algorithm. Like Dekker's algorithm, Peterson's algorithm requires three additional mailboxes. One mailbox is used to hold a turn message, either "It's Jill's turn" or "It's Bill's turn." Each representative uses a separate mailbox to make requests to access the order mailbox (i.e., to request use of the critical section). When a representative wishes to enter the critical section, their request is set to "yes." Initially, neither representative is requesting entrance to the CS.

STEP	INSTRUCTIONS
A:	Sell.
B:	Set my request to "yes."
C:	Set turn to favor the other representative.
D:	If the other representative has requested entry to the CS and
E:	If it is the other representative's turn, then go to D.
F:	(CS) Leave an order message and wait for it to be picked up.
G:	Set my request to "no" and go back to selling (go to A).

Initial conditions: Jill's request = Bill's request = "no" Turn = Jill's

Figure 5.11   Algorithm 7 — Peterson's Algorithm

Peterson's algorithm has all of the features of Dekker's algorithm: (1) guaranteed mutual exclusion of the critical section, (2) no deadlock, and (3) guaranteed progress. This is seen by examining the state transition diagram (see Exercise 5). Under the given conditions, the throughput of Peterson's algorithm is 4.334 encyclopedia sets sold per hour, an improvement of 3% over Dekker's algorithm and 10% over Algorithm 2. Under a heavy workload when the time to make a sale is 1 minute, Peterson's algorithm delivers a throughput of 6.574, which, although still not as good as Algorithm 2 (i.e., 7.466), is superior to Dekker's algorithm (i.e., 5.432).

The significance of these examples is not trivial. In the design of operating systems, choices must be made. Often, several different algorithms are possible to manage a particular resource. Some of the possibilities can be discarded immediately because they do not have certain desired properties. However, often several feasible alternatives exist. Simple analysis, such as done here, can (1) compare the various alternatives directly and quantitatively, and (2) identify those workloads in which each alternative performs best. This suggests new hybrid approaches based on thresholds. When the workload intensity is below some given threshold, one algorithm should be used by the operating system. As the workload intensity increases above the threshold, another algorithm should be used. Finding the appropriate thresholds is one of the purposes of the performance evaluation techniques presented in these examples.

5.9 CONCLUSIONS

Table 5.1 shows the results of the analyses of all seven algorithms. Of the seven, Algorithm 2 (turn-passing), Algorithm 6 (Dekker's), and Algorithm 7 (Peterson's) are the only acceptable candidates. Each guarantees mutual exclusion, freedom from deadlock, and progress. Peterson's algorithm is preferred to Dekker's because it delivers better performance in all cases due to reduced overhead. For the parameters specified in the encyclopedia problem, Peterson's algorithm is preferred over the turn-passing algorithm because it exhibits higher throughput. However, for systems with high demand on the critical section, the simple turn-passing algorithm is preferred. In these situations the overhead required by Peterson's algorithm becomes a bottleneck.

TABLE 5.1 Comparison of Results

Algorithm	Mutual Exclusion	Deadlock Free	Guaranteed Progress	"Given" System Throughput	"High-Demand" System Throughput
1. Original	No	Yes	Yes	—	—
2. Turn passing	Yes	Yes	Yes	3.954	7.466
3. Voting I	No	Yes	Yes	—	—
4. Voting II	Yes	No	No	—	—
5. Voting III	Yes	Yes	No	4.406	5.890
6. Dekker's	Yes	Yes	Yes	4.192	5.432
7. Peterson's	Yes	Yes	Yes	4.334	6.574

EXERCISES

1. ** Construct the state diagram for the original algorithm, Algorithm 1, and show that this algorithm is not acceptable.

2. *** Analyze the following suggested hybrid algorithm. Bill's behavior follows that of Algorithm 3 and Jill's behavior follows that of Algorithm 4. Draw the appropriate state diagram and address the issues of mutual exclusion, deadlock, guaranteed progress, and throughput.

3. **** Analyze Algorithm 5 and verify that the throughput is 4.406 encyclopedia sets sold per hour.

4. **** Analyze Algorithm 2 and Algorithm 5 under the "high-demand" case when the sales rate is 60 instead of 4. Verify that in this case, Algorithm 2 outperforms Algorithm 5. At which sales rate (somewhere between 4 and 60) do Algorithm 2 and Algorithm 5 exhibit the same performance (i.e., what is the demand threshold at which Algorithm 2 and Algorithm 5 have the same performance)?

5. ** Draw the complete state transition diagram for Peterson's algorithm.

6. **** Write a program that generates the states and transitions of Dekker's and Peterson's algorithms. Use this information to set up the system of balance equations and solve them using an appropriate solution package.

7. *** Find that demand threshold (i.e., that rate at which encyclopedia sets are sold) which causes Algorithm 2 and Peterson's algorithm to have the same performance. Thus if the demand is greater than this threshold value, Algorithm 2 is better. If the demand is less than this threshold value, Peterson's algorithm performs better.

8. **** Modern operating systems run on hardware that provides a test-and-set operation, by which semaphores are implemented. Develop several alternative solutions to the producers/consumers problem using semaphores and compare their performance under different workloads. Develop an alternative solution to the producers/consumers problem using semaphores and compare its performance to that of Algorithms 2, 5 and 6 when the sales rate is 4 and 60.

chapter six

Memory Management

PROBLEM

Most print shops offer, among other things, business card printing. There are many different styles and colors from which to choose. The time it takes to change inks (i.e., colors) on a press is very long compared with the actual time it takes to print a single order. Therefore, print shops change colors on a daily basis. For example, on Monday all the black-ink business cards are printed, on Tuesday all the red-ink cards are printed, and so on. The drawback is that a customer placing a business card order may have to wait several days for printing—until the color desired recycles.

The operating system counterpart is a pure demand paging virtual memory system. There are five pages of virtual memory (five colors) and two page frames of physical memory (two presses). If a page is not in physical memory, a page fault occurs (one of the presses must be recast and loaded with a different color). Choosing which resident page to replace with the requested page is done according to the page replacement policy. This problem compares various page replacement policies given the frequency with which different pages are referenced. The objective is to minimize the probability that the next memory reference will cause a page fault.

NiftyPrint hopes to corner the business card market by specializing in business cards and offering service "while you wait." To do this, NiftyPrint will offer only five colors: *a*, *b*, *c*, *d*, and *e*. Each shop will be equipped with two identical presses, each loaded with a different color. Therefore, if a customer walks in and places an order using one of the loaded colors, that customer is serviced virtually instantaneously. However, if a customer places an order for one of the three colors that is not loaded, one of the presses will have to be recast for that color, which takes a long time.

Some colors are more popular than others.

Some pages of memory are more frequently referenced than others. For example, the page containing the main computation loop of a program will be referenced more often than the page containing the startup code. The concepts of working set and locality are closely related to the study of page replacement strategies.

The popularity of a color *x* can be expressed as the probability p_x that *x* is the next requested color. For example, p_a is the probability that color *a* is requested next, and p_e is the probability that color *e* is requested next. If all colors (*a*, *b*, *c*, *d*, *e*) are equally popular, the corresponding probability distribution would be $(\frac{1}{5}, \frac{1}{5}, \frac{1}{5}, \frac{1}{5}, \frac{1}{5})$. Similarly, if color *a* is twice as popular as all other colors, the corresponding distribution would be $(\frac{1}{3}, \frac{1}{6}, \frac{1}{6}, \frac{1}{6}, \frac{1}{6})$.

In situations where the color requested is not loaded on either press, four ways for choosing which press to recast have been suggested

---

[the four page replacement strategies compared are RANDOM, FIFO (i.e., LTI), LRU, and an anticipatory scheme (i.e., LP)]:

- *Random (RANDOM).* The press operator flips a coin to decide which press to recast.
- *Longest-time-in (LTI).* The color that has been loaded for the longest time is the one to be replaced.
- *Least-recently-used (LRU).* The press that was not used on the last print job is the one to be recast.

- *Least-popular (LP)*. The press containing the least popular color is recast. If both colors are equally popular, a press is chosen at random.

For each of the five following popularity distributions $\mathcal{D}_i, i = 1 \cdots 5$, compare the four replacement algorithms. The objective is to minimize the probability that a customer must wait for a press to be recast to the desired color.

$$\mathcal{D}_1 = (0.2, 0.2, 0.2, 0.2, 0.2)$$
$$\mathcal{D}_2 = (0.6, 0.1, 0.1, 0.1, 0.1)$$
$$\mathcal{D}_3 = (0.35, 0.35, 0.1, 0.1, 0.1)$$
$$\mathcal{D}_4 = (0.3, 0.3, 0.3, 0.05, 0.05)$$
$$\mathcal{D}_5 = (0.5, 0.2, 0.2, 0.05, 0.05)$$

6.1 NOTATION

Throughout this section the following notation is used:

- p_x: probability that color x is requested next, where x is either a, b, c, d, or e.
- $\mathcal{D} = (p_a, p_b, p_c, p_d, p_e)$: probability distribution of color popularity. A particular color distribution is denoted using a subscript (e.g., $\mathcal{D}_i$).
- xy: a state, where x and y are the two colors currently loaded. For the RANDOM and LP (least-popular) algorithms, xy and yx are equivalent. For LTI (longest-time-in) xy indicates that x has been in the longest. For LRU (least-recently-used), xy indicates that y is the least recently used color.
- $\mathcal{S}$: set of all possible states.
- P_{xy}: probability of being in state xy.

6.2 APPLICATION TO OPERATING SYSTEMS

The corresponding operating systems problem is known as the *page replacement* problem. Computer systems that use virtual memory can provide programs with address spaces that are many times larger than the actual amount of physical memory available.* As a program runs, it generates references to pages of vir-

---

*It is assumed that the reader is familiar with basic virtual memory concepts.

tual memory that it wishes to access. A reference string is a list of the pages the program references in the order in which they are referenced. If a program references a page that is not currently resident in primary memory, a page fault occurs. Before the program can continue execution, the operating system selects a page currently in primary memory to be replaced by the referenced page. That is, as a result of the fault, the operating system must first select a page that is in memory to be replaced with the requested page. This page fault overhead is relatively costly. The problem is to determine the page replacement algorithm that results in the lowest overhead cost.

In the current analogy, different ink colors correspond to the different pages of virtual memory. The two presses correspond to page frames. The event in which a customer requests business cards of a color that is not currently loaded corresponds to a page fault. The color popularity distributions represent typical page reference behavior. In previous problems, the objective has been to maximize throughput or to minimize response time. In this problem the objective is to minimize the probability that a page fault will occur on any given memory reference. The page fault rate directly affects other performance metrics, such as throughput and response time.

Something else is unique about this problem: Nowhere is the word "rate" mentioned. In earlier examples, the rate of flow across an arc in a state transition diagram depended on the probability of being in that state and the rate at which the event triggering the transition occurred. In this problem the occurrence of an event (i.e., a change in state) is triggered by a probability, which is the popularity of a color. That is, the analysis is rate independent.

Actually, the difference here is that, in previous problems, *continuous transition* Markov processes have been used. That is, state changes can occur at any time and one gets the sense that the system "flows" from state to state (hence the words "flow rate"). In the solution to this problem, *discrete transition* Markov processes are used. State changes occur only at certain times—when a customer enters. The new state is chosen based on a probability distribution. The bottom line is that both methods are effectively equivalent. As shown, the analysis technique is the same.

For example, suppose that colors a and e are currently loaded on the two presses and the popularity distribution of colors is $\mathcal{D}_3 = (0.35, 0.35, 0.1, 0.1, 0.1)$. Assume that the replacement algorithm is RANDOM. This means that the current state is ae and that $p_a = p_b = 0.35$ and $p_c = p_d = p_e = 0.1$. As long as color a or color e is the next color requested, the state of the system does not change. Therefore, the probability that the state does not change is $p_a + p_e = 0.35 + 0.1 = 0.45$. However, if the next color is not a or e, the state will change. The probability of this occurring is $p_b + p_c + p_d = 0.35 + 0.1 + 0.1 = 0.55$

(which is also equal to $1 - p_a - p_e$, since the sum of all probabilities must be equal to 1). If b is the next color, one of the presses will have to be recast (i.e., a fault occurs). Since the replacement algorithm is RANDOM, there is a 50% probability that the press currently loaded with color a will be recast and a 50% probability that the press currently loaded with e will be recast. Therefore, if b is the next color, either state ab or be will be entered. The probability of entering state ab is $p_b \times 0.5 = 0.35 \times 0.5 = 0.175$. Similarly, the probability of entering state be is 0.175. Figure 6.1 shows all possible transitions out of state ae under the RANDOM replacement policy.

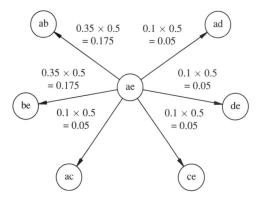

Figure 6.1 Arcs departing state ae under the RANDOM policy

Given the entire state transition diagram for a specific replacement algorithm, the derivation of the system of balance equations and the solution for each color distribution is relatively straightforward. This yields the steady-state probabilities for each of the states for each of the color distributions. Since the "arc rates" are restricted to be probabilities, the "flows" across arcs represent the probabilities of state changes. Each state change corresponds to a fault. Thus the total flow rate across the arcs out of a state yields the probability that a fault will occur when the system is in that state. The desire is to construct a table of the fault probabilities given an algorithm and color distribution.

6.3 RANDOM POLICY

Now let's analyze the RANDOM policy in detail.

In the RANDOM page replacement policy, whenever a page fault occurs, a random page from main memory is selected for replacement.

Each state is designated by the two colors that are currently loaded on the presses. The order of colors in the state label is not important. For example, state xy is the same as state yx. For consistency, colors will be given alphabetically (i.e., state xy instead of yx). Since there are five colors and only two of them can be loaded at any time, we can determine the total number of possible states by computing the number of combinations:

$$\binom{5}{2}, \quad \text{which is} \quad \frac{5!}{2!\,(5-2)!} = 10.$$

Each state will have $3 \times 2 = 6$ arcs departing it. That is, either of the two loaded colors could be replaced by one of the three nonloaded colors. Therefore, the state transition diagram for RANDOM has 10 states and 60 arcs.

Drawing the state diagram is tedious due to the large number of arcs. It is not a lot of fun and does not yield much insight into the problem. Sometimes it is better and easier to provide a transition matrix instead of the diagram. The transition matrix for the RANDOM policy is given in Table 6.1. This is an N by N matrix, where N is the number of states (in this case, $N = 10$). The rows and columns are indexed by the state label. The value stored at row i column j is the label of the arc that leads from state i to state j. This represents the probability of leaving state i and entering state j when a customer enters the print shop. A blank entry indicates that there is no arc between the states. Each diagonal entry represents a self-loop in which a customer enters the store to find that the desired color is already loaded on a press. The existence (or nonexistence) of self-loops does not affect the solution since self-loops represent both flow-in and flow-out of the same states. These flows "cancel" each other. Not only are transition matrices better for representing large diagrams, but the balance equations are easier to write down. Indeed, the process is automatic, and a simple program can be written to generate the matrix and the corresponding equations. (That's what we did!) The drawback to using a transition matrix is that the visual impression and intuition of how the states interact is lost. It is more difficult to look at a transition matrix and get a feeling for how the system behaves.

Let S be the set of all possible states. That is,

$$S = \{ab, ac, ad, ae, bc, bd, be, cd, ce, de\}$$

Generating the balance equations from the transition matrix is pretty easy. Consider some state $i \in S$ for which the flow-in and flow-out are to be calculated (i.e., a balance equation is to be derived). The flow out of state i is the sum $P_i \sum_j M(i, j)$ and the flow into state i is the sum $\sum_j P_j M(j, i)$, where $M(x, y)$ is the value at row x column y of the transition matrix, P_x is the probability of being in state x, and j ranges over all states in S. Therefore, the balance

TABLE 6.1   State transition matrix for the RANDOM policy

	ab	ac	ad	ae	bc	bd	be	cd	ce	de
ab	†	$\frac{p_c}{2}$	$\frac{p_d}{2}$	$\frac{p_e}{2}$	$\frac{p_c}{2}$	$\frac{p_d}{2}$	$\frac{p_e}{2}$			
ac	$\frac{p_b}{2}$	†	$\frac{p_d}{2}$	$\frac{p_e}{2}$	$\frac{p_b}{2}$			$\frac{p_d}{2}$	$\frac{p_e}{2}$	
ad	$\frac{p_b}{2}$	$\frac{p_c}{2}$	†	$\frac{p_e}{2}$		$\frac{p_b}{2}$		$\frac{p_c}{2}$		$\frac{p_e}{2}$
ae	$\frac{p_b}{2}$	$\frac{p_c}{2}$	$\frac{p_d}{2}$	†			$\frac{p_b}{2}$		$\frac{p_c}{2}$	$\frac{p_d}{2}$
bc	$\frac{p_a}{2}$	$\frac{p_a}{2}$			†	$\frac{p_d}{2}$	$\frac{p_e}{2}$	$\frac{p_d}{2}$	$\frac{p_e}{2}$	
bd	$\frac{p_a}{2}$		$\frac{p_a}{2}$		$\frac{p_c}{2}$	†	$\frac{p_e}{2}$	$\frac{p_c}{2}$		$\frac{p_e}{2}$
be	$\frac{p_a}{2}$			$\frac{p_a}{2}$	$\frac{p_c}{2}$	$\frac{p_d}{2}$	†		$\frac{p_c}{2}$	$\frac{p_d}{2}$
cd		$\frac{p_a}{2}$	$\frac{p_a}{2}$		$\frac{p_b}{2}$	$\frac{p_b}{2}$		†	$\frac{p_e}{2}$	$\frac{p_e}{2}$
ce		$\frac{p_a}{2}$		$\frac{p_a}{2}$	$\frac{p_b}{2}$		$\frac{p_b}{2}$	$\frac{p_d}{2}$	†	$\frac{p_d}{2}$
de			$\frac{p_a}{2}$	$\frac{p_a}{2}$		$\frac{p_b}{2}$	$\frac{p_b}{2}$	$\frac{p_c}{2}$	$\frac{p_c}{2}$	†

† Diagonal elements indicate the probability of going from state xy to state xy (i.e., a self-loop) whenever a customer enters the print shop. This is simply the probability that the color requested is already loaded — $p_x + p_y$. Since self-loops do not affect the solution, these probabilities are not explicitly given in the table. Note that when self-loops are included, each row must sum to 1.

equation for state i is

$$\overbrace{P_i \sum_{j \in \mathcal{S}} M(i, j)}^{\textit{flow-out}} = \overbrace{\sum_{j \in \mathcal{S}} P_j M(j, i)}^{\textit{flow-in}}, \quad i \in \mathcal{S}$$

The system of equations for the RANDOM replacement policy is

$$P_{ab}\left(\frac{p_c}{2} + \frac{p_d}{2} + \frac{p_e}{2} + \frac{p_c}{2} + \frac{p_d}{2} + \frac{p_e}{2}\right)$$
$$= P_{ac}\frac{p_b}{2} + P_{ad}\frac{p_b}{2} + P_{ae}\frac{p_b}{2} + P_{bc}\frac{p_a}{2} + P_{bd}\frac{p_a}{2} + P_{be}\frac{p_a}{2}$$
$$P_{ac}\left(\frac{p_b}{2} + \frac{p_d}{2} + \frac{p_e}{2} + \frac{p_b}{2} + \frac{p_d}{2} + \frac{p_e}{2}\right)$$
$$= P_{ab}\frac{p_c}{2} + P_{ad}\frac{p_c}{2} + P_{ae}\frac{p_c}{2} + P_{bc}\frac{p_a}{2} + P_{cd}\frac{p_a}{2} + P_{ce}\frac{p_a}{2}$$

$$P_{ad}\left(\frac{p_b}{2} + \frac{p_c}{2} + \frac{p_e}{2} + \frac{p_b}{2} + \frac{p_c}{2} + \frac{p_e}{2}\right)$$

$$= P_{ab}\frac{p_d}{2} + P_{ac}\frac{p_d}{2} + P_{ae}\frac{p_d}{2} + P_{bd}\frac{p_a}{2} + P_{cd}\frac{p_a}{2} + P_{de}\frac{p_a}{2}$$

$$P_{ae}\left(\frac{p_b}{2} + \frac{p_c}{2} + \frac{p_d}{2} + \frac{p_b}{2} + \frac{p_c}{2} + \frac{p_d}{2}\right)$$

$$= P_{ab}\frac{p_e}{2} + P_{ac}\frac{p_e}{2} + P_{ad}\frac{p_e}{2} + P_{be}\frac{p_a}{2} + P_{ce}\frac{p_a}{2} + P_{de}\frac{p_a}{2}$$

$$P_{bc}\left(\frac{p_a}{2} + \frac{p_a}{2} + \frac{p_d}{2} + \frac{p_e}{2} + \frac{p_d}{2} + \frac{p_e}{2}\right)$$

$$= P_{ab}\frac{p_c}{2} + P_{ac}\frac{p_b}{2} + P_{bd}\frac{p_c}{2} + P_{be}\frac{p_c}{2} + P_{cd}\frac{p_b}{2} + P_{ce}\frac{p_b}{2}$$

$$P_{bd}\left(\frac{p_a}{2} + \frac{p_a}{2} + \frac{p_c}{2} + \frac{p_e}{2} + \frac{p_c}{2} + \frac{p_e}{2}\right)$$

$$= P_{ab}\frac{p_d}{2} + P_{ad}\frac{p_b}{2} + P_{bc}\frac{p_d}{2} + P_{be}\frac{p_d}{2} + P_{cd}\frac{p_b}{2} + P_{de}\frac{p_b}{2}$$

$$P_{be}\left(\frac{p_a}{2} + \frac{p_a}{2} + \frac{p_c}{2} + \frac{p_d}{2} + \frac{p_c}{2} + \frac{p_d}{2}\right)$$

$$= P_{ab}\frac{p_e}{2} + P_{ae}\frac{p_b}{2} + P_{bc}\frac{p_e}{2} + P_{bd}\frac{p_e}{2} + P_{ce}\frac{p_b}{2} + P_{de}\frac{p_b}{2}$$

$$P_{cd}\left(\frac{p_a}{2} + \frac{p_a}{2} + \frac{p_b}{2} + \frac{p_b}{2} + \frac{p_e}{2} + \frac{p_e}{2}\right)$$

$$= P_{ac}\frac{p_d}{2} + P_{ad}\frac{p_c}{2} + P_{bc}\frac{p_d}{2} + P_{bd}\frac{p_c}{2} + P_{ce}\frac{p_d}{2} + P_{de}\frac{p_c}{2}$$

$$P_{ce}\left(\frac{p_a}{2} + \frac{p_a}{2} + \frac{p_b}{2} + \frac{p_b}{2} + \frac{p_d}{2} + \frac{p_d}{2}\right)$$

$$= P_{ac}\frac{p_e}{2} + P_{ae}\frac{p_c}{2} + P_{bc}\frac{p_e}{2} + P_{be}\frac{p_c}{2} + P_{cd}\frac{p_e}{2} + P_{de}\frac{p_c}{2}$$

$$P_{de}\left(\frac{p_a}{2} + \frac{p_a}{2} + \frac{p_b}{2} + \frac{p_b}{2} + \frac{p_c}{2} + \frac{p_c}{2}\right)$$

$$= P_{ad}\frac{p_e}{2} + P_{ae}\frac{p_d}{2} + P_{bd}\frac{p_e}{2} + P_{be}\frac{p_d}{2} + P_{cd}\frac{p_e}{2} + P_{ce}\frac{p_d}{2}$$

$$\sum_{x\in S} P_x = 1$$

Don't forget this last equation since one of the equations in any stochastic matrix is redundant.

We could solve this system of equations leaving $p_a \cdots p_e$ as free variables. However, this gets a little messy, and substituting actual values for $p_a \cdots p_e$ before performing the solution will make the solution easier, just not as general.

First, consider the assignment $\mathcal{D}_1 = (0.2, 0.2, 0.2, 0.2, 0.2)$, in which all colors are equally popular. Solving the equations is really easy in this case and the steady-state probability of being in any state is $\frac{1}{10}$. This is not surprising because all colors are equally popular. No color is given preferential treatment by the RANDOM policy with respect to when that color was loaded or last used. Therefore, the probability of being in any state is the same as being in any other state. We can also solve the system of equations for each of the other four distributions $\mathcal{D}_2 \cdots \mathcal{D}_5$. The results of these solutions are given in Table 6.2.

TABLE 6.2 Steady-state probabilities for the RANDOM policy

	$\mathcal{D}_1$	$\mathcal{D}_2$	$\mathcal{D}_3$	$\mathcal{D}_4$	$\mathcal{D}_5$
P_{ab}	$\frac{1}{10}$	$\frac{1}{5}$	$\frac{49}{145}$	$\frac{36}{145}$	$\frac{40}{133}$
P_{ac}	$\frac{1}{10}$	$\frac{1}{5}$	$\frac{14}{145}$	$\frac{36}{145}$	$\frac{40}{133}$
P_{ad}	$\frac{1}{10}$	$\frac{1}{5}$	$\frac{14}{145}$	$\frac{6}{145}$	$\frac{10}{133}$
P_{ae}	$\frac{1}{10}$	$\frac{1}{5}$	$\frac{14}{145}$	$\frac{6}{145}$	$\frac{10}{133}$
P_{bc}	$\frac{1}{10}$	$\frac{1}{30}$	$\frac{14}{145}$	$\frac{36}{145}$	$\frac{16}{133}$
P_{bd}	$\frac{1}{10}$	$\frac{1}{30}$	$\frac{14}{145}$	$\frac{6}{145}$	$\frac{4}{133}$
P_{be}	$\frac{1}{10}$	$\frac{1}{30}$	$\frac{14}{145}$	$\frac{6}{145}$	$\frac{4}{133}$
P_{cd}	$\frac{1}{10}$	$\frac{1}{30}$	$\frac{4}{145}$	$\frac{6}{145}$	$\frac{4}{133}$
P_{ce}	$\frac{1}{10}$	$\frac{1}{30}$	$\frac{4}{145}$	$\frac{6}{145}$	$\frac{4}{133}$
P_{de}	$\frac{1}{10}$	$\frac{1}{30}$	$\frac{4}{145}$	$\frac{1}{145}$	$\frac{1}{133}$

We now have sufficient information to calculate the probability that one of the presses must be recast whenever a customer enters the shop (i.e., the probability of a fault occurring). In the state transition diagram, *any* change in state is the result of a fault. Think about it: Whenever the state changes from, say, state ab to ac, this is the result of recasting the second press from having color b to having color c. Therefore, the goal is to stay in the same state as long as possible. Thus the sum of the flows of all arcs departing (excluding self-looping arcs, by which the state does not change) gives the probability that a fault occurs. An easy way to do this is to sum the flow out of all states. This sum of flow out of all states for the RANDOM replacement policy is

$$P_{ab}\left(\frac{p_c}{2}+\cdots+\frac{p_e}{2}\right)+\cdots+P_{de}\left(\frac{p_a}{2}+\cdots+\frac{p_c}{2}\right)$$

which is equal to

$$P_{ab}\left(p_c+p_d+p_e\right)+\cdots+P_{de}\left(p_a+p_b+p_c\right)$$

Consider color distribution $\mathcal{D}_2$, where $p_a = \frac{3}{5}$ and $p_b = p_c = p_d = p_e = \frac{1}{10}$ and where $P_{ab} = P_{ac} = P_{ad} = P_{ae} = 1/5$ and $P_{bc} = P_{bd} = P_{be} = P_{cd} = P_{ce} = P_{de} = \frac{1}{30}$ (see Table 6.3). The sum of the flow out of all states is

$$4\left[\frac{1}{5}\left(\frac{1}{10}+\frac{1}{10}+\frac{1}{10}\right)\right]+6\left[\frac{1}{30}\left(\frac{3}{5}+\frac{1}{10}+\frac{1}{10}\right)\right]=\frac{2}{5}$$

This means that under the RANDOM policy with color distribution $\mathcal{D}_2$, there is a 40% chance that the next request will cause a fault. Table 6.3 shows the fault probabilities of all color distributions.

TABLE 6.3 Fault
probabilities for the
RANDOM policy

Distribution	Fault Prob.
$\mathcal{D}_1$	0.600
$\mathcal{D}_2$	0.400
$\mathcal{D}_3$	0.486
$\mathcal{D}_4$	0.466
$\mathcal{D}_5$	0.417

6.4 LONGEST-TIME-IN-POLICY

When a fault occurs under the LTI (longest-time-in) policy, the decision of which color should be changed is easy: It is always the one that has been loaded on a press the longest. This is the same as saying that colors are swapped out in the order in which they were loaded.

The page replacement policy analyzed here is the first-in-first-out policy (FIFO). Whenever a page fault occurs, the "oldest" page in main memory is selected for replacement.

With only two presses, this implies that the presses are recast in a strictly alternating pattern. For example, suppose that colors c and e are currently loaded, with e being the color last loaded. If a request for a comes in, c is swapped out and a takes its place. If a request for b comes in next, e will be swapped out, and so on. A request for a color that is already loaded does not affect how "old" that color is (i.e., the length of time since the color was originally loaded). The "age" of a color depends strictly on when it was loaded.

How many states and arcs are in the state transition diagram for LTI? (Try to figure this out before reading further.) Only two of five colors can be loaded at any time. From the calculation of the number of states in RANDOM, this yields

$$\binom{5}{2} = 10$$

states. However, if two colors are loaded, either one of them can be the oldest color. This information must be "remembered" in the state of the system. Thus the total number of states for LTI is $2 \times 10 = 20$. Now examine the outgoing arcs for a typical state. To cause a fault, one of the three colors not loaded must be requested. Whenever a fault occurs, regardless of which color caused the fault, the same "remembered" color will be swapped out. Therefore, there are three outgoing arcs for every state. The total number of arcs is $3 \times 20 = 60$.

For the RANDOM policy, the states ab and ba were the same state. For LTI, however, these are distinct states, where the first color of the state label is the oldest. For example, ab is the state where colors a and b are loaded, with a being the oldest color. Similarly, state ba is the state where colors a and b are loaded, but b is the oldest color. The state transition matrix for LTI is given in Table 6.4. Although not terribly exciting, yet included for completeness, the balance equations derived from the transition matrix are

$$P_{ab}(p_c + p_d + p_e) = P_{ca}p_b + P_{da}p_b + P_{ea}p_b$$

$$P_{ac}(p_b + p_d + p_e) = P_{ba}p_c + P_{da}p_c + P_{ea}p_c$$

$$P_{ad}(p_b + p_c + p_e) = P_{ba}p_d + P_{ca}p_d + P_{ea}p_d$$

$$P_{ae}(p_b + p_c + p_d) = P_{ba}p_e + P_{ca}p_e + P_{da}p_e$$

$$P_{ba}(p_c + p_d + p_e) = P_{cb}p_a + P_{db}p_a + P_{eb}p_a$$

$$P_{bc}(p_a + p_d + p_e) = P_{ab}p_c + P_{db}p_c + P_{eb}p_c$$

$$P_{bd}(p_a + p_c + p_e) = P_{ab}p_d + P_{cb}p_d + P_{eb}p_d$$

TABLE 6.4 State transition matrix for the LTI policy

	ab	ac	ad	ae	ba	bc	bd	be	ca	cb	cd	ce	da	db	dc	de	ea	eb	ec	ed
ab						p_c	p_d	p_e												
ac										p_b	p_d	p_e								
ad														p_b	p_c	p_e				
ae																		p_b	p_c	p_d
ba		p_c	p_d	p_e																
bc									p_a		p_d	p_e								
bd													p_a		p_c	p_e				
be																	p_a		p_c	p_d
ca	p_b		p_d	p_e																
cb					p_a		p_d	p_e												
cd													p_a	p_b		p_e				
ce																	p_a	p_b		p_d
da	p_b	p_c		p_e																
db					p_a	p_c		p_e												
dc									p_a	p_b		p_e								
de																	p_a	p_b	p_c	
ea	p_b	p_c	p_d																	
eb					p_a	p_c	p_d													
ec									p_a	p_b	p_d									
ed													p_a	p_b	p_c					

134

$$P_{be}(p_a + p_c + p_d) = P_{ab}p_e + P_{cb}p_e + P_{db}p_e$$

$$P_{ca}(p_b + p_d + p_e) = P_{bc}p_a + P_{dc}p_a + P_{ec}p_a$$

$$P_{cb}(p_a + p_d + p_e) = P_{ac}p_b + P_{dc}p_b + P_{ec}p_b$$

$$P_{cd}(p_a + p_b + p_e) = P_{ac}p_d + P_{bc}p_d + P_{ec}p_d$$

$$P_{ce}(p_a + p_b + p_d) = P_{ac}p_e + P_{bc}p_e + P_{dc}p_e$$

$$P_{da}(p_b + p_c + p_e) = P_{bd}p_a + P_{cd}p_a + P_{ed}p_a$$

$$P_{db}(p_a + p_c + p_e) = P_{ad}p_b + P_{cd}p_b + P_{ed}p_b$$

$$P_{dc}(p_a + p_b + p_e) = P_{ad}p_c + P_{bd}p_c + P_{ed}p_c$$

$$P_{de}(p_a + p_b + p_c) = P_{ad}p_e + P_{bd}p_e + P_{cd}p_e$$

$$P_{ea}(p_b + p_c + p_d) = P_{be}p_a + P_{ce}p_a + P_{de}p_a$$

$$P_{eb}(p_a + p_c + p_d) = P_{ae}p_b + P_{ce}p_b + P_{de}p_b$$

$$P_{ec}(p_a + p_b + p_d) = P_{ae}p_c + P_{be}p_c + P_{de}p_c$$

$$P_{ed}(p_a + p_b + p_c) = P_{ae}p_d + P_{be}p_d + P_{ce}p_d$$

$$\sum_{x \in S} P_x = 1$$

As with RANDOM, any change of state is triggered by a fault. Therefore, the probability of a fault occurring is the sum of the flows across all arcs. Substituting values for $p_a \cdots p_e$ for each distribution $\mathcal{D}_1 \cdots \mathcal{D}_5$ and solving the system of equations will yield the steady-state probabilities for each state for each distribution. These are shown in Table 6.5. The state probabilities are then used to find the fault probability. The fault probabilities for each color distribution are given in Table 6.6. The fault probability is the sum of the flow out of all states, which is

$$P_{ab}(p_c + p_d + p_e) + \cdots + P_{ed}(p_a + p_b + p_c)$$

(i.e., the sum of the left-hand sides of the balance equations). But something seems to be wrong—these are exactly the same probabilities as those obtained for the RANDOM policy! This suggests that the extra state information kept by LTI (which color is oldest) is not important to the performance of the system.

This is both interesting and important. It has been independently observed in actual paging systems that FIFO page replacement schemes appear to perform no better than random replacement schemes. Thus, including *when* a page is replaced in the page table descriptors is an extra overhead activity that provides no performance improvement.

TABLE 6.5 Steady-state probabilities for the LTI policy

	$\mathcal{D}_1$	$\mathcal{D}_2$	$\mathcal{D}_3$	$\mathcal{D}_4$	$\mathcal{D}_5$
P_{ab}	$\frac{1}{20}$	$\frac{1}{10}$	$\frac{49}{290}$	$\frac{18}{145}$	$\frac{20}{133}$
P_{ac}	$\frac{1}{20}$	$\frac{1}{10}$	$\frac{7}{145}$	$\frac{18}{145}$	$\frac{20}{133}$
P_{ad}	$\frac{1}{20}$	$\frac{1}{10}$	$\frac{7}{145}$	$\frac{3}{145}$	$\frac{5}{133}$
P_{ae}	$\frac{1}{20}$	$\frac{1}{10}$	$\frac{7}{145}$	$\frac{3}{145}$	$\frac{5}{133}$
P_{ba}	$\frac{1}{20}$	$\frac{1}{10}$	$\frac{49}{290}$	$\frac{18}{145}$	$\frac{20}{133}$
P_{bc}	$\frac{1}{20}$	$\frac{1}{60}$	$\frac{7}{145}$	$\frac{18}{145}$	$\frac{8}{133}$
P_{bd}	$\frac{1}{20}$	$\frac{1}{60}$	$\frac{7}{145}$	$\frac{3}{145}$	$\frac{2}{133}$
P_{be}	$\frac{1}{20}$	$\frac{1}{60}$	$\frac{7}{145}$	$\frac{3}{145}$	$\frac{2}{133}$
P_{ca}	$\frac{1}{20}$	$\frac{1}{10}$	$\frac{7}{145}$	$\frac{18}{145}$	$\frac{20}{133}$
P_{cb}	$\frac{1}{20}$	$\frac{1}{60}$	$\frac{7}{145}$	$\frac{18}{145}$	$\frac{8}{133}$
P_{cd}	$\frac{1}{20}$	$\frac{1}{60}$	$\frac{2}{145}$	$\frac{3}{145}$	$\frac{2}{133}$
P_{ce}	$\frac{1}{20}$	$\frac{1}{60}$	$\frac{2}{145}$	$\frac{3}{145}$	$\frac{2}{133}$
P_{da}	$\frac{1}{20}$	$\frac{1}{10}$	$\frac{7}{145}$	$\frac{3}{145}$	$\frac{5}{133}$
P_{db}	$\frac{1}{20}$	$\frac{1}{60}$	$\frac{7}{145}$	$\frac{3}{145}$	$\frac{2}{133}$
P_{dc}	$\frac{1}{20}$	$\frac{1}{60}$	$\frac{2}{145}$	$\frac{3}{145}$	$\frac{2}{133}$
P_{de}	$\frac{1}{20}$	$\frac{1}{60}$	$\frac{2}{145}$	$\frac{1}{290}$	$\frac{1}{266}$
P_{ea}	$\frac{1}{20}$	$\frac{1}{10}$	$\frac{7}{145}$	$\frac{3}{145}$	$\frac{5}{133}$
P_{eb}	$\frac{1}{20}$	$\frac{1}{60}$	$\frac{7}{145}$	$\frac{3}{145}$	$\frac{2}{133}$
P_{ec}	$\frac{1}{20}$	$\frac{1}{60}$	$\frac{2}{145}$	$\frac{3}{145}$	$\frac{2}{133}$
P_{ed}	$\frac{1}{20}$	$\frac{1}{60}$	$\frac{2}{145}$	$\frac{1}{290}$	$\frac{1}{266}$

TABLE 6.6 Fault
probabilities for the LTI
policy

Distribution	Fault Prob.
$\mathcal{D}_1$	0.600
$\mathcal{D}_2$	0.400
$\mathcal{D}_3$	0.486
$\mathcal{D}_4$	0.466
$\mathcal{D}_5$	0.417

6.5 LEAST-RECENTLY-USED-POLICY

The LRU (least-recently-used) policy is similar to longest-time-in (LTI) in that when a fault occurs, the "oldest" color is swapped out. The difference is in the interpretation of "oldest." In the LTI sense, "oldest" refers to the time since a color was loaded. In the LRU sense, "oldest" refers to the time since a color was used. For example, under LRU, if a and b are the currently loaded colors and A is the oldest color (i.e., state ab), a request for a will *not* cause a fault, but it *will* cause a change in state (i.e., the new state will be state ba). A request for the youngest color will not cause a change in state. For example, if the current state is ab and a request for b occurs, there is neither a fault nor a change in state. The oldest color is the least-recently-used color and is the one to be swapped out in the event of a fault. The partial state diagram of Figure 6.2 shows this behavior with respect to states ab and ba.

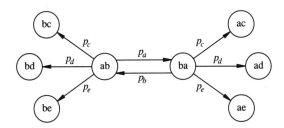

Figure 6.2   Partial state diagram for the LRU policy

Again, there are 20 states in the complete LRU state diagram, for exactly the same reasons there are 20 states in the LTI diagram. However, there are more arcs under LRU since (as shown above) one can change state without faulting. As illustrated in Figure 6.2, there are four outgoing arcs for each state, for a total of 80 arcs in the diagram. The state transition matrix for LRU is given in Table 6.7 and the resulting balance equations are

$$P_{ab}(p_a + p_c + p_d + p_e) = P_{ba}p_b + P_{ca}p_b + P_{da}p_b + P_{ea}p_b$$

$$P_{ac}(p_a + p_b + p_d + p_e) = P_{ba}p_c + P_{ca}p_c + P_{da}p_c + P_{ea}p_c$$

$$P_{ad}(p_a + p_b + p_c + p_e) = P_{ba}p_d + P_{ca}p_d + P_{da}p_d + P_{ea}p_d$$

$$P_{ae}(p_a + p_b + p_c + p_d) = P_{ba}p_e + P_{ca}p_e + P_{da}p_e + P_{ea}p_e$$

$$P_{ba}(p_b + p_c + p_d + p_e) = P_{ab}p_a + P_{cb}p_a + P_{db}p_a + P_{eb}p_a$$

$$P_{bc}(p_a + p_b + p_d + p_e) = P_{ab}p_c + P_{cb}p_c + P_{db}p_c + P_{eb}p_c$$

$$P_{bd}(p_a + p_b + p_c + p_e) = P_{ab}p_d + P_{cb}p_d + P_{db}p_d + P_{eb}p_d$$

$$P_{be}(p_a + p_b + p_c + p_d) = P_{ab}p_e + P_{cb}p_e + P_{db}p_e + P_{eb}p_e$$

$$P_{ca}(p_b + p_c + p_d + p_e) = P_{ac}p_a + P_{bc}p_a + P_{dc}p_a + P_{ec}p_a$$

$$P_{cb}(p_a + p_c + p_d + p_e) = P_{ac}p_b + P_{bc}p_b + P_{dc}p_b + P_{ec}p_b$$

$$P_{cd}(p_a + p_b + p_c + p_e) = P_{ac}p_d + P_{bc}p_d + P_{dc}p_d + P_{ec}p_d$$

$$P_{ce}(p_a + p_b + p_c + p_d) = P_{ac}p_e + P_{bc}p_e + P_{dc}p_e + P_{ec}p_e$$

$$P_{da}(p_b + p_c + p_d + p_e) = P_{ad}p_a + P_{bd}p_a + P_{cd}p_a + P_{ed}p_a$$

$$P_{db}(p_a + p_c + p_d + p_e) = P_{ad}p_b + P_{bd}p_b + P_{cd}p_b + P_{ed}p_b$$

$$P_{dc}(p_a + p_b + p_d + p_e) = P_{ad}p_c + P_{bd}p_c + P_{cd}p_c + P_{ed}p_c$$

$$P_{de}(p_a + p_b + p_c + p_d) = P_{ad}p_e + P_{bd}p_e + P_{cd}p_e + P_{ed}p_e$$

$$P_{ea}(p_b + p_c + p_d + p_e) = P_{ae}p_a + P_{be}p_a + P_{ce}p_a + P_{de}p_a$$

$$P_{eb}(p_a + p_c + p_d + p_e) = P_{ae}p_b + P_{be}p_b + P_{ce}p_b + P_{de}p_b$$

$$P_{ec}(p_a + p_b + p_d + p_e) = P_{ae}p_c + P_{be}p_c + P_{ce}p_c + P_{de}p_c$$

$$P_{ed}(p_a + p_b + p_c + p_e) = P_{ae}p_d + P_{be}p_d + P_{ce}p_d + P_{de}p_d$$

$$\sum_{x \in \mathcal{S}} P_x = 1$$

Substituting specific values for $p_a \cdots p_e$ according to the five distributions $\mathcal{D}_1 \cdots \mathcal{D}_5$ and solving the system above yields the steady-state probabilities shown in Table 6.8.

TABLE 6.7 State transition matrix for the LRU policy

	ab	ac	ad	ae	ba	bc	bd	be	ca	cb	cd	ce	da	db	dc	de	ea	eb	ec	ed
ab					p_a	p_c	p_d	p_e												
ac									p_a	p_b	p_d	p_e								
ad													p_a	p_b	p_c	p_e				
ae																	p_a	p_b	p_c	p_d
ba	p_b	p_c	p_d	p_e																
bc									p_a	p_b	p_d	p_e								
bd													p_a	p_b	p_c	p_e				
be																	p_a	p_b	p_c	p_d
ca	p_b	p_c	p_d	p_e																
cb					p_a	p_c	p_d	p_e												
cd													p_a	p_b	p_c	p_e				
ce																	p_a	p_b	p_c	p_d
da	p_b	p_c	p_d	p_e																
db					p_a	p_c	p_d	p_e												
dc									p_a	p_b	p_d	p_e								
de																	p_a	p_b	p_c	p_d
ea	p_b	p_c	p_d	p_e																
eb					p_a	p_c	p_d	p_e												
ec									p_a	p_b	p_d	p_e								
ed													p_a	p_b	p_c	p_e				

TABLE 6.8 Steady-state probabilities for the LRU policy

	$\mathcal{D}_1$	$\mathcal{D}_2$	$\mathcal{D}_3$	$\mathcal{D}_4$	$\mathcal{D}_5$
P_{ab}	$\frac{1}{20}$	$\frac{1}{15}$	$\frac{49}{260}$	$\frac{9}{70}$	$\frac{1}{8}$
P_{ac}	$\frac{1}{20}$	$\frac{1}{15}$	$\frac{7}{180}$	$\frac{9}{70}$	$\frac{1}{8}$
P_{ad}	$\frac{1}{20}$	$\frac{1}{15}$	$\frac{7}{180}$	$\frac{3}{190}$	$\frac{1}{38}$
P_{ae}	$\frac{1}{20}$	$\frac{1}{15}$	$\frac{7}{180}$	$\frac{3}{190}$	$\frac{1}{38}$
P_{ba}	$\frac{1}{20}$	$\frac{3}{20}$	$\frac{49}{260}$	$\frac{9}{70}$	$\frac{1}{5}$
P_{bc}	$\frac{1}{20}$	$\frac{1}{90}$	$\frac{7}{180}$	$\frac{9}{70}$	$\frac{1}{20}$
P_{bd}	$\frac{1}{20}$	$\frac{1}{90}$	$\frac{7}{180}$	$\frac{3}{190}$	$\frac{1}{95}$
P_{be}	$\frac{1}{20}$	$\frac{1}{90}$	$\frac{7}{180}$	$\frac{3}{190}$	$\frac{1}{95}$
P_{ca}	$\frac{1}{20}$	$\frac{3}{20}$	$\frac{7}{130}$	$\frac{9}{70}$	$\frac{1}{5}$
P_{cb}	$\frac{1}{20}$	$\frac{1}{90}$	$\frac{7}{130}$	$\frac{9}{70}$	$\frac{1}{20}$
P_{cd}	$\frac{1}{20}$	$\frac{1}{90}$	$\frac{1}{90}$	$\frac{3}{190}$	$\frac{1}{95}$
P_{ce}	$\frac{1}{20}$	$\frac{1}{90}$	$\frac{1}{90}$	$\frac{3}{190}$	$\frac{1}{95}$
P_{da}	$\frac{1}{20}$	$\frac{3}{20}$	$\frac{7}{130}$	$\frac{3}{140}$	$\frac{1}{20}$
P_{db}	$\frac{1}{20}$	$\frac{1}{90}$	$\frac{7}{130}$	$\frac{3}{140}$	$\frac{1}{80}$
P_{dc}	$\frac{1}{20}$	$\frac{1}{90}$	$\frac{1}{90}$	$\frac{3}{140}$	$\frac{1}{80}$
P_{de}	$\frac{1}{20}$	$\frac{1}{90}$	$\frac{1}{90}$	$\frac{1}{380}$	$\frac{1}{380}$
P_{ea}	$\frac{1}{20}$	$\frac{3}{20}$	$\frac{7}{130}$	$\frac{3}{140}$	$\frac{1}{20}$
P_{eb}	$\frac{1}{20}$	$\frac{1}{90}$	$\frac{7}{130}$	$\frac{3}{140}$	$\frac{1}{80}$
P_{ec}	$\frac{1}{20}$	$\frac{1}{90}$	$\frac{1}{90}$	$\frac{3}{140}$	$\frac{1}{80}$
P_{ed}	$\frac{1}{20}$	$\frac{1}{90}$	$\frac{1}{90}$	$\frac{1}{380}$	$\frac{1}{380}$

Knowing the steady-state probabilities, the probability of a fault occurring can be calculated. However, unlike the RANDOM and LTI systems, not all arc traversals are triggered by a fault. A transition from some state xy to state yx (its "twin") is not due to a fault. Therefore, the fault probability is found by summing only three of the four outgoing arcs of every state, ignoring the arc that goes to the twin state. The expression for the fault probability is

$$P_{ab}(p_c + p_d + p_e) + \cdots + P_{ed}(p_a + p_b + p_c)$$

The fault probability for each color distribution is given in Table 6.9.

TABLE 6.9 Fault
probabilities for the LRU
policy

Distribution	Fault Prob.
$\mathcal{D}_1$	0.600
$\mathcal{D}_2$	0.366
$\mathcal{D}_3$	0.472
$\mathcal{D}_4$	0.458
$\mathcal{D}_5$	0.398

6.6 LEAST-POPULAR POLICY

When a fault occurs under the least-popular (LP) policy, the color to be swapped out is the least popular color loaded, according to the distribution $\mathcal{D}_i$. If the two loaded colors are equally popular, one is chosen at random (i.e., there is a 0.5 probability that each color will be chosen).

The state transition diagram has 10 states; for the same reasons there are 10 states in the RANDOM diagram. That is, which two colors are currently loaded is important, but not the order in which those colors were loaded (i.e., state xy and state yx are the same state). The methodology for analyzing the LP policy is the same as before. However, things are a bit more involved here because the number of arcs in the diagram depends on the color distribution. For example, if all colors have different probabilities, there will never be a tie. In this case there is exactly one outgoing arc per possible fault per state. This yields a diagram with 30 arcs. At the other extreme, if all colors are equally popular (as is the case with distribution $\mathcal{D}_1$), there will always be a tie, meaning two arcs for each possible fault. This yields a diagram with 60 arcs (and is, incidentally, exactly the same as RANDOM under distribution $\mathcal{D}_1$).

Therefore, to solve for all five distributions, five different state transition matrices are needed. The state transition matrices for distributions $\mathcal{D}_1 \cdots \mathcal{D}_5$ are given in Tables 6.10 to 6.14. Since the derivation of the balance equations is straightforward, they are not given here for the sake of space. (You are probably not excited about looking at more equations, anyway.) The steady-state solutions are given in Table 6.15. As with RANDOM and LTI, whenever any arc is traversed under the LP policy, it is due to a fault. Therefore, the sum of the flow-outs for each state yields the probability of a fault occurring. These results are given in Table 6.16.

TABLE 6.10   State transition matrix for LP/$\mathcal{D}_1$

	ab	ac	ad	ae	bc	bd	be	cd	ce	de
ab		$\frac{p_c}{2}$	$\frac{p_d}{2}$	$\frac{p_e}{2}$	$\frac{p_c}{2}$	$\frac{p_d}{2}$	$\frac{p_e}{2}$			
ac	$\frac{p_b}{2}$		$\frac{p_d}{2}$	$\frac{p_e}{2}$	$\frac{p_b}{2}$			$\frac{p_d}{2}$	$\frac{p_e}{2}$	
ad	$\frac{p_b}{2}$	$\frac{p_c}{2}$		$\frac{p_e}{2}$		$\frac{p_b}{2}$		$\frac{p_c}{2}$		$\frac{p_e}{2}$
ae	$\frac{p_b}{2}$	$\frac{p_c}{2}$	$\frac{p_d}{2}$				$\frac{p_b}{2}$		$\frac{p_c}{2}$	$\frac{p_d}{2}$
bc	$\frac{p_a}{2}$	$\frac{p_a}{2}$				$\frac{p_d}{2}$	$\frac{p_e}{2}$	$\frac{p_d}{2}$	$\frac{p_e}{2}$	
bd	$\frac{p_a}{2}$		$\frac{p_a}{2}$		$\frac{p_c}{2}$		$\frac{p_e}{2}$	$\frac{p_c}{2}$		$\frac{p_e}{2}$
be	$\frac{p_a}{2}$			$\frac{p_a}{2}$	$\frac{p_c}{2}$	$\frac{p_d}{2}$			$\frac{p_c}{2}$	$\frac{p_d}{2}$
cd		$\frac{p_a}{2}$	$\frac{p_a}{2}$		$\frac{p_b}{2}$	$\frac{p_b}{2}$			$\frac{p_e}{2}$	$\frac{p_e}{2}$
ce		$\frac{p_a}{2}$		$\frac{p_a}{2}$	$\frac{p_b}{2}$		$\frac{p_b}{2}$	$\frac{p_d}{2}$		$\frac{p_d}{2}$
de			$\frac{p_a}{2}$	$\frac{p_a}{2}$		$\frac{p_b}{2}$	$\frac{p_b}{2}$	$\frac{p_c}{2}$	$\frac{p_c}{2}$	

TABLE 6.11   State transition matrix for LP/$\mathcal{D}_2$

	ab	ac	ad	ae	bc	bd	be	cd	ce	de
ab		p_c	p_d	p_e						
ac	p_b		p_d	p_e						
ad	p_b	p_c		p_e						
ae	p_b	p_c	p_d							
bc	$\frac{p_a}{2}$	$\frac{p_a}{2}$				$\frac{p_d}{2}$	$\frac{p_e}{2}$	$\frac{p_d}{2}$	$\frac{p_e}{2}$	
bd	$\frac{p_a}{2}$		$\frac{p_a}{2}$		$\frac{p_c}{2}$		$\frac{p_e}{2}$	$\frac{p_c}{2}$		$\frac{p_e}{2}$
be	$\frac{p_a}{2}$			$\frac{p_a}{2}$	$\frac{p_c}{2}$	$\frac{p_d}{2}$			$\frac{p_c}{2}$	$\frac{p_d}{2}$
cd		$\frac{p_a}{2}$	$\frac{p_a}{2}$		$\frac{p_b}{2}$	$\frac{p_b}{2}$			$\frac{p_e}{2}$	$\frac{p_e}{2}$
ce		$\frac{p_a}{2}$		$\frac{p_a}{2}$	$\frac{p_b}{2}$		$\frac{p_b}{2}$	$\frac{p_d}{2}$		$\frac{p_d}{2}$
de			$\frac{p_a}{2}$	$\frac{p_a}{2}$		$\frac{p_b}{2}$	$\frac{p_b}{2}$	$\frac{p_c}{2}$	$\frac{p_c}{2}$	

TABLE 6.12 State transition matrix for LP/$\mathcal{D}_3$

	ab	ac	ad	ae	bc	bd	be	cd	ce	de
ab		$\frac{p_c}{2}$	$\frac{p_d}{2}$	$\frac{p_e}{2}$	$\frac{p_c}{2}$	$\frac{p_d}{2}$	$\frac{p_e}{2}$			
ac	p_b		p_d	p_e						
ad	p_b	p_c		p_e						
ae	p_b	p_c	p_d							
bc	p_a					p_d	p_e			
bd	p_a				p_c		p_e			
be	p_a				p_c	p_d				
cd		$\frac{p_a}{2}$	$\frac{p_a}{2}$		$\frac{p_b}{2}$	$\frac{p_b}{2}$			$\frac{p_e}{2}$	$\frac{p_e}{2}$
ce		$\frac{p_a}{2}$		$\frac{p_a}{2}$	$\frac{p_b}{2}$		$\frac{p_b}{2}$	$\frac{p_d}{2}$		$\frac{p_d}{2}$
de			$\frac{p_a}{2}$	$\frac{p_a}{2}$		$\frac{p_b}{2}$	$\frac{p_b}{2}$	$\frac{p_c}{2}$	$\frac{p_c}{2}$	

TABLE 6.13 State transition matrix for LP/$\mathcal{D}_4$

	ab	ac	ad	ae	bc	bd	be	cd	ce	de
ab		$\frac{p_c}{2}$	$\frac{p_d}{2}$	$\frac{p_e}{2}$	$\frac{p_c}{2}$	$\frac{p_d}{2}$	$\frac{p_e}{2}$			
ac	$\frac{p_b}{2}$		$\frac{p_d}{2}$	$\frac{p_e}{2}$	$\frac{p_b}{2}$			$\frac{p_d}{2}$	$\frac{p_e}{2}$	
ad	p_b	p_c		p_e						
ae	p_b	p_c	p_d							
bc	$\frac{p_a}{2}$	$\frac{p_a}{2}$				$\frac{p_d}{2}$	$\frac{p_e}{2}$	$\frac{p_d}{2}$	$\frac{p_e}{2}$	
bd	p_a				p_c		p_e			
be	p_a				p_c	p_d				
cd		p_a			p_b				p_e	
ce		p_a			p_b			p_d		
de			$\frac{p_a}{2}$	$\frac{p_a}{2}$		$\frac{p_b}{2}$	$\frac{p_b}{2}$	$\frac{p_c}{2}$	$\frac{p_c}{2}$	

TABLE 6.14   State transition matrix for LP/$\mathcal{D}_5$

	ab	ac	ad	ae	bc	bd	be	cd	ce	de
ab		p_c	p_d	p_e						
ac	p_b		p_d	p_e						
ad	p_b	p_c		p_e						
ae	p_b	p_c	p_d							
bc	$\frac{p_a}{2}$	$\frac{p_a}{2}$				$\frac{p_d}{2}$	$\frac{p_e}{2}$	$\frac{p_d}{2}$	$\frac{p_e}{2}$	
bd	p_a				p_c		p_e			
be	p_a				p_c	p_d				
cd		p_a			p_b				p_e	
ce		p_a			p_b			p_d		
de			$\frac{p_a}{2}$	$\frac{p_a}{2}$		$\frac{p_b}{2}$	$\frac{p_b}{2}$	$\frac{p_c}{2}$	$\frac{p_c}{2}$	

TABLE 6.15   Steady-state probabilities for the LP policy

	$\mathcal{D}_1$	$\mathcal{D}_2$	$\mathcal{D}_3$	$\mathcal{D}_4$	$\mathcal{D}_5$
P_{ab}	$\frac{1}{10}$	$\frac{1}{4}$	$\frac{7}{13}$	$\frac{2}{7}$	$\frac{2}{5}$
P_{ac}	$\frac{1}{10}$	$\frac{1}{4}$	$\frac{1}{13}$	$\frac{2}{7}$	$\frac{2}{5}$
P_{ad}	$\frac{1}{10}$	$\frac{1}{4}$	$\frac{1}{13}$	$\frac{1}{42}$	$\frac{1}{10}$
P_{ae}	$\frac{1}{10}$	$\frac{1}{4}$	$\frac{1}{13}$	$\frac{1}{42}$	$\frac{1}{10}$
P_{bc}	$\frac{1}{10}$	0	$\frac{1}{13}$	$\frac{2}{7}$	0
P_{bd}	$\frac{1}{10}$	0	$\frac{1}{13}$	$\frac{1}{42}$	0
P_{be}	$\frac{1}{10}$	0	$\frac{1}{13}$	$\frac{1}{42}$	0
P_{cd}	$\frac{1}{10}$	0	0	$\frac{1}{42}$	0
P_{ce}	$\frac{1}{10}$	0	0	$\frac{1}{42}$	0
P_{de}	$\frac{1}{10}$	0	0	0	0

TABLE 6.16 Fault
probabilities for the LP
policy

Distribution	Fault Prob.
$\mathcal{D}_1$	0.600
$\mathcal{D}_2$	0.300
$\mathcal{D}_3$	0.415
$\mathcal{D}_4$	0.436
$\mathcal{D}_5$	0.330

6.7 COMPARISON OF THE POLICIES

Table 6.17 summarizes the fault probabilities for each policy and each color distribution.

Primary observations:

- This again illustrates that a simple state diagram approach can be used to compare various policies uniformly.
- If all pages are equally likely to be referenced, all policies give the same performance.
- RANDOM and LTI policies are the same—LTI offers no advantage over RANDOM and has higher overhead.
- *Generally,* when the page reference behavior favors certain pages (i.e., as the variance within the page reference distribution increases), performance improves. This is due to the fact that it is more likely that the next referenced page is already in memory.
- Policies that favor page reference locality (e.g., LRU) perform better than a random policy.
- Policies that are anticipatory (i.e., LP) perform better than other policies.
- Significant performance improvements are possible by using a good page replacement policy.

The color distributions are ordered by increasing variance within each distribution. The bottom row of the table shows the maximum percentage of improvement (i.e., reduction) of the fault probability over the RANDOM policy. The table indicates that when all colors are equally popular (i.e., the variance of the color distribution is zero), the choice of replacement policy is not important. As the variance of the color distribution increases, the choice of policy

TABLE 6.17 Comparison of all policies

Distribution	$\mathcal{D}_1$	$\mathcal{D}_4$	$\mathcal{D}_3$	$\mathcal{D}_5$	$\mathcal{D}_2$
Variance	0	0.15	0.15	0.27	0.400
		Fault probability			
RANDOM	0.600	0.466	0.486	0.417	0.400
LTI	0.600	0.466	0.486	0.417	0.400
LRU	0.600	0.458	0.472	0.398	0.366
LP	0.600	0.436	0.415	0.330	0.300
Max. % improvement over RANDOM	0%	6%	15%	20%	25%

becomes more important. In all cases, RANDOM and LTI perform identically and give the worst performance, LP gives the best performance, and LRU gives performance that is between RANDOM/LTI and LP. Therefore, LP is the most desirable policy regardless of the distribution. If the variance of the color popularity is high, using the LP policy can significantly improve performance.

6.8 STOCHASTIC ANALYSIS VS. SIMULATION

Throughout this book, the analysis has focused on a stochastic approach. The analysis of page replacement policies given in this chapter is no different. Using a probability distribution to describe the reference string allows steady-state analysis. However, for each of the five distributions examined, there are many specific reference strings that fall into each distribution. For example, the following reference strings all belong to distribution $\mathcal{D}_1$.

$$a, a, b, b, c, c, d, d, e, e, a, a, b, b, \ldots$$
$$a, b, c, d, e, a, b, c, d, e, a, b, c, d, \ldots$$
$$a, a, e, b, b, c, d, d, e, c, a, a, e, b, \ldots$$
$$a, a, \ldots, b, b \ldots, c, c, \ldots, d, d, \ldots, e, e, \ldots$$

Each policy yields different performance for each of these strings, even though they all belong to the same distribution. Another way to analyze the performance of a policy is to describe a specific reference string explicitly rather than probabilistically. The specific reference string may have come from actual measurement trace data. The next color to be referenced is deterministic (i.e., the next color is known since it is the color that occurs next in the reference string) rather than probabilistic.

To compare policies, one would "run" the same reference string on each policy and record the fault probability (i.e., the ratio of fault occurrences to the total number of references). The policy causing the least number of faults is considered best with respect to that reference string. This type of analysis is a simple instance of *simulation*. Although simulation has been ignored in this book, it is, nonetheless, an important analysis technique. As a matter of fact, simulation is one of the most popular performance evaluation techniques. A simulator is a program that simulates the system's behavior and keeps up with the number of times different events occur. For example, the following is a simulator written in C for the LTI policy:

```c
#include <stdio.h>
    main() {
        char press1=' '; /* the color loaded on press 1    */
        char press2=' '; /* the color loaded on press 2    */
        char nextcolor;  /* next color referenced          */
        int faults=0;    /* number of faults (counter)     */
        int totalrefs=0; /* number of references (counter) */

        while ( (nextcolor=getchar()) != EOF )
          if (nextcolor>='a' && nextcolor<='e') {
            /* ignore spaces, commas, etc */
            totalrefs++;
            if (nextcolor!=press1 && nextcolor!=press2) {
              /* a fault has occurred */
              faults++;
              press1=press2;
              press2=nextcolor;
            }
          }
        printf("Fault percentage: %8.5f\n",
               100.0*(faults/totalrefs));
    }
```

The simulator reads characters from an input file. The file represents the reference string being analyzed. When the end of the input is reached, the simulation is over, and the fault probability is computed and printed out. The fault probabilities reported for the four sample reference strings above are 50%, 100%, 70%, and 0%, respectively. This indicates the diversity of results that can be obtained and that the true fault percentage depends critically on the assumed input workload characteristics.

The major drawbacks to simulation are (1) the amount of time required to write the simulation program (even though the simulator above is easy to write, general simulators can be quite complex), and (2) the amount of time it takes to run the simulator to ensure an equivalent of steady-state behavior (usually, simulators calculate "confidence intervals" which indicate the statistical significance of their results), and (3) the difficulty in obtaining appropriate trace data. There are several languages and software packages that provide a high-level user interface for writing simulations. (You would not want to write a C program every time you wanted to run a different simulation.) These packages minimize the time required to construct simulation programs. Simulations can provide almost any desired level of detail, but the additional detail increases the potential for errors (i.e., there is just a lot more to be sure to get right).

So which is better: stochastic analysis or simulation? The answer: it depends on the objective. Stochastic analysis often gives better insight into the nature of a problem and is more flexible when comparing several alternatives at a high level. Simulation is more general (i.e., requires fewer assumptions) and can obtain exact statistics for any specific trace. A good performance analyst is familiar with and uses both techniques according to the context of the problem being solved.

EXERCISES

6.1 ** Analyze "shortest-time-in" (STI) where the page replaced is the one that has been in the press the shortest amount of time (this is equivalent to last-in-first-out). Assume that color c is the first referenced color. Compare this policy with the four policies analyzed in this section.

6.2 *** Analyze "most-popular" (MP). Compare this policy with the four policies analyzed in this section. Can you characterize those policies that will do worse than RANDOM?

6.3 **** Give the balance equations for the five distributions ($\mathcal{D}_1 \cdots \mathcal{D}_5$) for the LP policy. Solve them and verify the solution against Table 6.15.

6.4 *** Let $\mathcal{D}_6 = (0.05, 0.10, 0.15, 0.25, 0.45)$. Perform the analysis and add in the appropriate column in Table 6.17 for $\mathcal{D}_6$. How are the policy rankings affected by this distribution?

6.5 *** Suppose now that there are three presses (i.e., page frames). Perform the analysis using $\mathcal{D}_2$ for the four policies and make appropriate comparisons and observations.

6.6 **** Suppose that there are fewer colors (i.e., pages). What effect would this have on the comparisons? Justify your answers by replacing p_d with $p_d + p_e$, replacing p_e with zero, and performing the appropriate analysis.

6.7 **** Write simulation programs for each of the four page replacement policies and experiment with different reference strings, including the four given in Section 6.8.

6.8 **** Adapt the simulation programs written in Exercise 7 to analyze the probabilistic distributions $\mathcal{D}_1 \cdots \mathcal{D}_5$. Each program will need to generate random numbers according to the distribution being simulated. Compare the results with those shown in Table 6.17.

6.9 ** Are the RANDOM and LTI policies *really* equivalent? If so, prove it. If not, describe a specific situation in which they will not yield the same performance.

6.10 *** Consider the policy LP/LRU, which is the same as LP except in the case of ties (i.e., when the two loaded colors have the same probability). When a tie occurs, the rules of LRU are used to break the tie. Since LRU performed better than RANDOM, one would expect LP/LRU to perform better than LP (where ties are broken as in RANDOM). Is this the case? Justify your claim by solving this policy for each distribution.

6.11 **** *Locality* refers to the tendency for a program in execution to reference a selected set of pages, called the *working set*. Suppose that the probability of other colors being requested changes based on the last color requested. Consider, for example, that when the last referenced color is a, $\mathcal{D} = (0.4, 0.1, 0.1, 0.1, 0.3)$; when the last color is b, $\mathcal{D} = (0.2, 0.5, 0.2, 0.05, 0.05)$; when the last color is c, $\mathcal{D} = (0.1, 0.2, 0.3, 0.2, 0.2)$; when the last color is d, $\mathcal{D} = (0.05, 0.1, 0.2, 0.5, 0.15)$; and when the last color is e, $\mathcal{D} = (0.3, 0.05, 0.05, 0.1, 0.5)$. Construct the state transition diagrams for this example under each policy. Compare the number of states and arcs with the diagrams of the original problem. Solve this policy and compare it to those in the chapter. Consider a system in which the distribution $\mathcal{D}$ depends on the last *two* colors referenced and the order in which they were referenced. Speculate on the number of states and arcs in the corresponding diagrams.

Afterword

As stated in the preface, the goal of this book is to "increase the performance awareness and to improve the performance modeling skills" of the readers. The single modeling technique used throughout the book is that of state diagrams. This approach has been used in a variety of situations comparing a variety of different alternatives. This technique has proven to be surprisingly useful and versatile. Mastery and confidence in applying this simple approach leads to a quick (and sometimes dirty) analysis of many situations. However, the quantitative and qualitative insights provided are both valid and important. The goal of increasing performance awareness and improving performance modeling skills can be achieved by applying simple techniques.

Other approaches could have been selected to achieve the same objective. These include measurement case studies, more traditional stochastic analysis techniques, performance bounding techniques, Petri net models, and others. Any of these approaches, when applied consistently, are equally effective. The use of these other approaches is planned in sequel books. Besides, in any good design, one has to leave room for future innovation and improvement.

Bibliography

BASKETT, F., K. M. CHANDY, R. R. MUNTZ, and F. G. PALACIOS, "Open, closed, and mixed networks of queues with different classes of customers," *Journal of the Association for Computing Machinery* 22, 2(April 1975), 248–260.

DENNING, P. J., and J. P. BUZEN, "The operational analysis of queueing network models," *Computing Surveys* 10, 3(September 1978), 225–261.

KANT, K. Introduction to Computer System Performance Evaluation. McGraw-Hill, New York, 1992.

KLEINROCK, L. Queueing Systems, Volume 1: Theory. Wiley, New York, 1975.

LAZOWSKA, E. D., J. ZAHORJAN, G. S. GRAHAM, and K. C. SEVCIK, Quantitative System Performance: Computer System Analysis Using Queueing Network Models. Prentice Hall, Englewood Cliffs, N.J., 1984.

LITTLE, J. D. C. "A proof of the queueing formula $L = \lambda W$," *Operations Research* 9, 3(1961), 383–387.

MOLLOY, M. K. Fundamentals of Performance Modeling. Macmillan, New York, 1989.

TRIVEDI, K. S. Probability and Statistics with Reliability, Queueing and Computer Science Applications. Prentice Hall, Englewood Cliffs, N.J., 1982.

Index

A

Address space 125
Anticipatory paging 124, 145
Arrival rate 7, 10, 15
Arrival time 7, 10

B

Balance equation 15, 26, 27, 30, 31,
    34, 37, 39, 109, 111, 113, 127,
    128, 133, 138
Bottleneck 8, 114, 118
Buffer 4, 5, 7, 25

C

C-LOOK (see Disk scheduling)
Communication (see Process)
Context switch 67, 69, 73, 82, 83

Continuous transition 126
CPU 3, 5, 8, 13, 23, 53, 79, 104
CPU scheduling 23, 52, 57
    FCFS (First-Come-First-Serve) 52,
        54, 58, 70, 72, 73
    LCFS (Last-Come-First-Serve) 52,
        58, 61, 69, 70, 72, 73
    LJF (Longest-Job-First) 52, 57, 60,
        70, 72
    preemptive 58, 82, 83
    PS (Processor-Sharing) 67–70, 72,
        73
    RR (Round-Robin) 52, 62, 67, 68,
        70, 72, 73
    SJF (Shortest-Job-First) 52, 58, 60,
        70, 72
Critical section 106, 108, 109, 113,
    114, 118
C-SCAN (see Disk scheduling)
Cylinder 79, 81, 82, 85

D

Deadlock 103, 112, 113, 115

157

lect. 10/12-10/14
OSC ch.6 159-167
PSOS Ch.5